Wicca Crystals Book

Book

Starting with Crystals and Gemstones with this Step by Step Guide. Learn about Wicca Healing Stones and Everything You Need to Know (2022 Guide for Beginners)

Trina Quinn

Table of Contents

Introduction

1st Chapter: Crystals and Stones in History

- Energy Uses, Earthly Magic
- Traditional Spiritual, Purposeful Practice

2nd Chapter: Crystals and Their Mysteries

- Jade
- Carnelian
- Amethyst
- Quartz
- Rose Quartz
- Citrine
- Malachite
- Hematite
- Moonstone
- Bloodstone
- Jet
- Tiger's Eye
- Lapis Lazuli
- Other

3rd Chapter: From Projective to Receptive, the Magic of Stones

- Masculine Energy: Projective Power
- Feminine Energy and Receptive Power

4th Chapter: The Best Crystals and Stones: How to Pick and Use The Best Crystals and Stones:

- How to Pick and Use
- Crystals for cleansing
- Crystals are being charged.
- Keeping crystals safe

5th Chapter: Organizing and Maintaining Good Power with the Crystal Configuration

- Altar of Crystals
- Grid of Crystals
- Ideas for a General Organization

6th Chapter: The Stone Garden: Organizing and Maintaining Good

- Wiccan Garden Power Stones and Crystals
- General Wiccan Garden Ideas

7th Chapter: Essences and Elixirs in Practical Magic

- The Crystal's Essence is its core.
- Elixirs are magical concoctions.
- Use of Potions in General

8th Chapter: Talismans and Amulets in Practical Magic

- Attractive Auras Talismans
- Shields of Protection: Amulets
- General Usage Advice

9th Chapter: Baths are an example of practical magic.

10th Chapter: Crystals and Candles for Practical Magic

- Grounding
- Health
- Love
- Joyfulness
- Abundance
- Success
- ESP
- Assistance with Sleeping

- <u>Stress Reduction</u>

<u>11th Chapter: Crystals and Herbs in Practical Magic</u>

<u>Conclusion</u>

Introduction

First and foremost, I want to express my gratitude for selecting Wicca Crystals Book. I'm confident that the knowledge on these pages will help you improve your magical practice.

The usage of crystals is one of the most important aspects of Wiccan practice: these ancient earth products and their essential ingredients are curiously alive, drawing energy from all realms. Wiccans use crystals for a variety of purposes, including cultivating love, generating positive energy, and providing protection. With their potential to link to global forces and bring them into your house and heart, gemstones and other stones are also important components of Wiccan practice. Throughout this book, you'll discover how to employ crystals and stones in your practice, often in conjunction with other Wiccan tools, for magical and practical outcomes.

The history of crystals and why these magical elements are used in practically every ritual, spell, and Wiccan home will be our first topic. Then we'll go through how to employ the various crystals in Wicca to assist you in achieving your goals. We'll learn why stones have been used as sources of immense power throughout human history, from productive tools to defensive weaponry, in the next chapter.

Then we'll look at how to pick the best stones and crystals, as well as how to utilize, store, and arrange them. Finally, we'll do some practice. Crystals are essential in the manufacture of a variety of other therapeutic potions that can improve health and well-being in a variety of formulas, in addition to channeling energies and directing intentions via altar settings and personal adornment.

1st Chapter:
Crystals and Stones in History

The usage of crystals and stones is inextricably linked to Wicca: these magical components appear in virtually every ceremony, nearly every spell, and in nearly every Wiccan home. Their abilities to create and channel beneficial energies that emerge directly from the earth, the Mother Goddess's source, are unrivaled. Crystals and other stones are commonly utilized in Wiccan and other pagan forms of magic, as well as in healing rituals and to increase the spiritual energy of certain areas.

Energy Uses, Earthly Magic

Technically, the crystals utilized in Wiccan magic are not all crystals; they are a set of solid minerals that have been lumped together under the term "crystal" for convenience. As a result, the terms "crystals" and "stones" are frequently interchanged, despite substantial categorical differences between the two groupings that will be discussed later in the book. Quartz, like rose quartz and amethyst, is a genuine crystal, the kind of ur-mineral from which all other crystals descended. Other crystal magic minerals, such as lapis lazuli, jade, and bloodstone, are actually mixtures of numerous elements and minerals, not pure crystals.

Regardless, they're all employed in Wiccan rituals, and each has its own unique energy and function. A full list of the most often utilized crystals and stones, as well as their qualities, may be found in Chapter 2.

Most Wiccans claim to be able to feel the energy emanating from powerful crystals. It is true that, despite being formed of inorganic, inert material, crystals can occasionally release a genuine electrical signal, known as the piezoelectric effect, when subjected to pressure, or a pyroelectric signal when subjected to temperature changes. As a result, it's not altogether out of the question to speculate that these elements contain a spark of universal energy, a flicker of purpose. In any case, their unique geometric configuration, link to earthly powers, and brilliant hues make them ideal for Wiccan magic and ritual. Not to mention the phantom energy signatures—other types of pagan practice

All energy, whether organic or inorganic, is interconnected and meaningful in Wiccan belief: the wind and the rushing of a river signify energy just as much as conscious life forms do. As a result, crystals are a part of this global energy. Furthermore, because our thoughts—our intentions—are energy, we may channel that energy through instruments like crystals and stones to transmit our wishes to a separate dimension, the spiritual realm. We're setting the intention, which is then channeled through the crystals' energy fields (and other magical tools) to produce some form of effect. There are still debates about the nature of consciousness: many people, including scientists, believe that consciousness is something separate from the physical presence of the brain; that is, awareness exists outside of our unique identities. As a result, when we use crystals, stones, and other Wiccan instruments, we are projecting and communicating with this consciousness that is woven into the fabric of the universe. Crystals and stones are mostly connected with healing and the ability to boost positivity by allowing more energy to flow between items and intentions.

These artifacts have been used for rituals and ceremonies from the dawn of time. Consider the massive Stonehenge construction, which has yet to be defined in terms of its strength; it's effectively a gigantic stone garden, similar to one you might build in your own backyard for power and defense. Consider the gem-encrusted adornments of kingdoms, warriors, and priests from antiquity to the present day; this isn't just a display of wealth—though that is the accepted, if incomplete, current view—but an age-old conviction that these earthly elements embody and represent power.

Even our popular imagination has been saturated by the association between crystals and magical powers; the Indiana Jones franchise has used the trope numerous times, from the first (the staff of Ra requires a crystal to map the Well of Souls) to an overt connection in the last, the Kingdom of the Crystal Skull. Of course, this is only one example among many, but it's particularly important given the religious undercurrent in these flicks. Crystals have been mentioned in history dating back to the Sumerians, and the ancient Egyptians used crystals and minerals extensively in their rituals—often as protective amulets, but also in make-up and other ritual decoration. Everyone from Greek sailors to Greek fighters used various stones for luck and protection in ancient Greece—our modern name derives from the Greek for "ice"—and everyone from Greek sailors to Greek warriors used various stones for luck and safety. The usage of valuable metals and stones can also be found throughout Asia; in China, jade was one of the most important, if not the most important, stones, with everything from musical instruments to body armor made of it.

Native American tribes in the United States and Mexico, as well as Maori tribes in New Zealand, have all employed crystals and stones for ornamentation, healing, and protection. The efficacy of earthly materials appears to have been acknowledged by a wide range of societies throughout history. Throughout history, both in the East and the West, religious invocations of crystals and stones have been widespread. Not only are precious stones mentioned in the Bible and the Koran, but they also have important religious significance in Hinduism and Buddhism. There are references to a diamond seat on which the Buddha would meditate—and, one could infer, connect to the universal consciousness—as well as the Kalpar Tree, a Hindu tribute to the gods made of valuable stones. In Hindu mythology, the diamond is linked to thunder and the goddess Indra's huge thunderbolt, which connects the ground and the heavens.

Rubies were thought to bring good fortune since they symbolized an unquenchable flame. Crystals and stones are undeniably important in all major world religions, as well as lesser belief systems, and their potency has long been recognized. As a result, it's clear that, while many mainstream ideologies mock crystal magic's "New Age" vibe, attributing it to fading hippies and other easily caricatured figures, they're missing out on the very real scientific evidence that reveals the hidden powers of inorganic materials and minerals of all kinds (think of pottery and the magnetic poles: the shift in the magnetism of our poles was discovered through the carbon dating of pottery). This is in addition to a better understanding of how the universe works as a result of quantum physics, which is still relatively recent (at least in scientific terms). Furthermore, this moderately unpleasant crystal caricature The very real history of the utilization of minerals and other natural materials to express power, money, status, and a whole host of other very real human thoughts and behaviors is also lost on gazers.

 Wiccans are simply more awakened and open to the possibilities offered by crystals and their ilk.

Traditional Spiritual, Purposeful Practice
In Wiccan practice, crystals and stones are used in a number of ways (see Chapters 2 and 3 for further detail on individual objects). When beginning ritual practice, one of the most common uses is to mark the sacred circle with crystals or stones. Another is to pay homage to the gods and goddesses, as different crystals and stones are associated with different gods and goddesses. Crystals and stones are also frequently utilized to adorn Wiccan practitioners' tools, altars, ritual clothes, and jewelry, owing to their natural energy channeling properties—these aren't merely aesthetic additions, but rather potent additions. These elements are utilized in Wiccan practice for healing, divination, and as talismans and amulets, among other things (see Chapters 7-11 for details on how crystals and stones are used in specific forms of magic).

A Wiccan practitioner can also learn how to "charge" a crystal with her intention and carry it with her to carry that energy with her wherever she goes. Crystals and stones can be found in a variety of venues, from New Age philosophy or Wiccan practice shops to natural mineral stores; there are also endless options online, however seasoned Wiccans will advise selecting them in person. Because crystals emit delicate energy and each human is susceptible to different energies in different ways, it's entirely conceivable to imply that the Wiccan picks the crystal rather than the other way around (as with the Harry Potter wands, no?).

The wizard is chosen by the wand). This is why it is advisable to choose crystals and stones in person. Color, in addition to energy, plays an important role in crystal selection, as it has its own magical characteristics; the tiny color changes in crystals can only be noticed up close. Advice on selecting and acquiring crystals and stones can be found in Chapter 4.Keep in mind some of the following general suggestions for how to effectively employ these magical things in your daily Wiccan life and practice, regardless of how you chose and use your crystals and stones.

- Before you utilize any crystal, be sure it has been cleansed. Any lingering energy that isn't to your taste should be washed away; start fresh to obtain the maximum value out of your intentions.
- Many Wiccans keep a crystal beside them at night, sometimes even beneath their pillow. Amethyst and selenite are both supposed to aid in relaxation and sleep, so they're wonderful options for that purpose. Some seasoned Wiccans even claim that specific

crystals can aid in remembering and interpreting dreams, which are powerful foreshadowing's of what is to come.

- Carry crystals with you, as previously stated. With a piece of citrine in your handbag or briefcase, you may travel with peace of mind, knowing that its protective properties are always with you.
- From your most mundane daily to-do list to your notebook to your list of spells and/or objectives, use crystals to improve the energy surrounding your actions. Keep your to-do list, desire list, intentions list—or all of the above—in a secure location with a crystal placed on top.
- The crystal's energy will infuse your lists with intention and purpose, ensuring that they will be completed. Not just for environments, but also for personal use, crystals are wonderful cleaners. For example, you can use crystals in the bath to encourage tranquility or look for mineral scrubs to get rid of negative energy. See Chapter 9 for further information.
- Crystals are excellent guides because of their tremendous energy. You may use crystals to literally direct energy from one location to another. You can direct the crystalline energy to a certain spot if you have a definite aim behind it.
- Remember to look for spells that will assist you in charging your crystals with specific intents and energies; they will need to be re-charged on a regular basis to retain their efficacy. Throughout the practical magic section of the book, there will be instructions on how to do this (Chapters 7-11).
- Crystals can be utilized to construct elixirs, talismans, healing baths, and candle and herbal magic, to name

a few examples from the Practical Magic chapters. They can be used to attract love, enhance harmony, give protection, deepen inner clarity, break negative habits, and assist you in achieving goals, among other things. Within Wiccan practice, they are truly vital instruments.

- Finally, remember to appreciate your crystals: the pleasant energy you infuse them with just strengthens them and makes you more effective. Crystals and stones are an important element of the self-care that your Wiccan practice allows you to cultivate.

2nd Chapter:
Crystals and Their Mysteries

As mentioned in the last chapter, crystals are widely used in Wiccan practice, and their energy can be quite powerful. Learning how to use the various crystals in Wicca will assist you in achieving your goals. In Chapter 4, you'll learn some fundamental guidelines for selecting and using crystals and stones in your practice. We'll have a look at the various crystals that are available and used in Wiccan rituals.

Jade

Jade is a sign of purity and tranquility that is thought to have magical properties all across the world, particularly in China and New Zealand (where the stone is commonly found). It was also highly valued in Mayan society, where it was utilized for both protection and ornamentation. Because green is an earth color that corresponds to the Mother Goddess, jade is highly treasured in numerous Wiccan rituals.

As such, jade is significant in healing, especially of plants and other natural components. It is thought to bring good fortune (green is frequently used).It is also said to aid in the formation of love relationships (symbolizes prosperity). The Chinese believed that jade might help them make critical judgments since it was a beneficial conduit to the brain. IN modern Wiccan practice, jade is used in ritual to protect the wearer. It can also be used to form a protective barrier around your garden. It is most commonly used to aid in healing: wearing jade near a wounded region of the physical body can channel healing energy toward that area, and it can also be used to cure non-physical wounds. The fundamental causes of sickness or psychic pain can be helped by wearing jade. You can also make a jade rosary, which can be used as "worry stones" when you need to feel calm and reassured.

Carnelian
The fire element is related with this dark stone with touches of crimson. It is used at the Samhain Sabbat in many places around the world, from India in the east to Britain in the west. In ancient Egypt, it was employed in both living and dead ceremonies (ancient Egyptian rituals for the dead were elaborate and intensely sacred). Carnelian was occasionally fashioned into the shape of a sword and set over the threshold as protection against the house during the Renaissance. Its ubiquity makes it easy to find and popular in spiritual practices all around the world. Carnelian is said to fortify the intellect; wearing it can

inspire boldness without being aggressive, and is especially beneficial for those who are afraid of public speaking. Carnelian is sometimes used to treat depression, anxiety, and addiction. Carnelian is said to help prevent blood illnesses and insanity by warming the blood (it is connected with fire, after all) (long thought to be the result of imbalances in the blood or humors). Because of its relationship to the fire element, it can also help you harness sexual energy. It can be employed in magic to protect against psyche attacks and to ward off bad enchantments. It's also a fantastic source of reviving sacred sites and positive energy, thanks to its fire element. Carnelian may stimulate passionate energy and powerful areas in the same way it can rouse the blood.

Amethyst

Amethyst actually means "not intoxicated" in etymology, as it was once thought that wearing amethyst would keep you from getting drunk. While this is probably not totally accurate, the connotations with safety remain. Its purple colour can range from barely visible to royal purple. It's a stone with a wide range of properties and is linked to the elements of air and water. Amethyst is a natural sedative with relaxing characteristics, as well as a mood stabilizer, dispersing anger, anxiety, and fear. It is one of the most popular stones in Wiccan practice. It is utilized for protection and cleaning as well as having great therapeutic properties. Amethyst, in the hands of trained practitioners, can aid with psychic channeling and intuition opening. The calming effect alluded to in its name essentially implies that amethyst is both a stimulant and a balm for the mind, stimulating positive psychic energy while soothing negative energies. Many Wiccans keep an amethyst stone by their bedside or under their pillow because it is thought to aid in the interpretation of dreams and the banishing of nightmares. Amethyst is a strong, practically all-purpose crystal that has the ability to channel energy and heal psychic issues.

Quartz

Quartz is the most basic and all-encompassing of crystals, representing all four elements and hence being utilized frequently in all Wiccan practices. It is possibly the truest of all crystals, in terms of chemical structure and represented via its clear, pure character. It's also very easy to get by, as it's one of the most common (some sources claim it's the most frequent) minerals on the planet, occurring on all continents except Antarctica. The name is derived from the Greek word for ice, as it was supposed that the gods created it from ice. Since at least the middle Ages, this is most likely the mineral material from which "crystal balls" have been made and used. Because of its versatility, every Wiccan will have at least one quartz crystal in her collection. There are other varieties of quartz (see below for Rose Quartz), and amethyst and onyx are two of them, both made of pure quartz with the addition of a number of other elements to generate the shape and color differences. Quartz has been proved to be receptive to energy by even materialist scientists; in studies, quartz has been shown to be electro-conductive and to have its own energy signal, giving it an almost biological appearance. As a result, whatever spell, ritual, or intention you cast will be successful. Quartz could be useful in various ways if you want to construct something. It basically enhances any type of energy that it receives or conducts, making it an essential tool in the Wiccan toolbox. It's also used for protection and healing, as are many crystals, and its color clarity is claimed to promote mental clarity. Keep a quartz crystal on your desk to help you stay focused in your life or at work if you have trouble staying focused. It's also a good idea to put a particularly powerful piece of quartz on your altar since, as previously said, it may help you with nearly any form of ritual.

Rose Quartz
As previously stated, this pale pink to pastel lavender stone is the most similar to pure quartz. It is associated with the Mother Goddess since it is tied to the earth and water signs. Rose quartz, like the Mother Goddess and her universal offspring, embodies the spirit and energy of completely unconditional love (nature and everything we experience in the world). If you want to concentrate your Wiccan practice on self-love or love in general, getting a few rose quartz crystals is a good option. Rose quartz is believed to consolidate friendship and

produce emotions of tranquility, in addition to being utilized in rituals to develop and enhance love. It has the ability to promote deep interior healing, such as that connected with broken hearts and unsettled minds. Rose quartz can help with heartache and loss of many kinds, as well as calming the mind and emotions during times of great grief. Rose quartz, in essence, removes emotional pollution while attracting serene and loving energy. This promotes forgiving and acceptance, both of oneself and others. Anyone suffering from depression or anxiety would benefit from having a few of these crystals on hand (in addition to consulting with a doctor or mental health professional). Make a necklace out of it to keep it close to your heart.

Citrine

Citrine has a gorgeous brownish-orange colour to it that varies in strength, but often of what is offered as citrine is actually amethyst or quartz that has been treated, so double-check your sourcing. Citrine looks a lot like the more expensive topaz and is occasionally sold as such, but citrine is a softer stone and hence more delicate, thus it should be handled with care. Citrine is known as "the success stone" or "the merchant stone," among other names. Citrine's qualities to channel good fortune, increase confidence, and attract money and abundance are indicated by these nicknames. To continue to attract additional riches, keep a citrine stone in your till or where you keep your savings (or put one in your handbag or wallet). Some believe that citrine is immune to bad energy and hence does not need to be cleansed, merely refilled from time to time. Citrine can also aid in the removal of toxins from the body, making it beneficial for digestive system cleansing. It is such a steadfastly positive stone that it may also be used to purify other stones, and as such, any Wiccan should have one in her collection. Use it to boost your self-esteem and bring joy into your life.

Malachite

Malachite is a lovely stone with interspersed whorls of varying colors of green and black that may be found all across Europe and the Middle East. Because it is such a soft stone, it is both easy to carve and easy to break; as a result, it should be treated with care. Malachite was frequently utilized to build ritual containers and as amulets for protection due to its auspicious green color and easily carved surface. Malachite was utilized by the ancient Greeks to safeguard their offspring, and it was considered that malachite could repel black magic in the middle Ages. Malachite can be used in both body and mind rituals and spells, and is particularly effective in increasing physical vitality. It can rejuvenate and revive cells, and is widely used in Eastern practice to re-energize the chakras. It is commonly worn throughout the body and can alleviate all types of inflammation, making it beneficial to the joints and circulatory system in general. It improves the immune system in general. Many people use malachite to prevent and relieve migraines because it shields them from annoying noise and undesirable electromagnetic radiation. In a state of meditation, contemplating the malachite stone helps to channel empathy and compassion, increasing feelings of harmony and patience. This also prepares the mind to accept positive energy by opening it up. It's commonly used to decorate a nursery since it can protect from bad intentions and nightmares. It should be recharged frequently and handled with care because it is a soft stone. For the gentlest recharging, place it atop clear quartz in warm—not hot—sunlight. It has a type of copper ore, thus it's worth looking into. Use caution when handling and avoid using in any spells or elixirs that require the substance to be consumed, since this can be harmful.

Hematite

Hematite is a rich black stone with overtones of steely silver, but it can also be reddish-brown in color. Its steely appearance connects it to fire and earth, and it's frequently used to boost willpower and strength. Soldiers in Ancient Rome used to apply this iron oxide stone over their bodies before battle because it was supposed to bring good luck (this was also, for practical purposes, very good camouflage in certain locations).It is most commonly used to boost willpower and should be utilized by those who want to kick bad habits like smoking, overeating, or drinking excessively. When attempting to predict the future, gazing into its nearly reflecting surface is also beneficial; it helps to re-direct energies toward the positive rather than the negative. It's known as a "mind stone," since it aids in improving our attention span, memory, and even sparking innovative thought. It helps to create a balance between the universal energies and your own bodily nerve system, and it does so in a particularly universal way. As a result, it's used to treat a wide range of compulsions, from addictions to anxiety. It also keeps your mind and body in tune with the spiritual realm by preventing you from absorbing external negativity.

Moonstone

While moonstone comes in a variety of colors, its luminous shade is most desirable when it is pale grey or

extremely light blue in color. It was supposed to be actual moonlight in crystallized form in ancient times. Moonstone is closely associated with the moon and its associations in Wiccan and other pagan practices, so it's no wonder that it's regarded the stone of real love and romance, as well as fertility. Moonstone encourages peaceful reconciliation between lovers, and when presented to a partner (during a full moon for best results), it ensures that the relationship will always be passionate. Its link to the moon also makes it a fantastic choice for encouraging prophetic dreams while eliminating nightmares; the moonstone soothes our sensitive emotions, allowing us to create our dreams and perform divination. Moonstone is a lucky stone that is also a protection stone for travelers, especially those who travel by sea or at night (again, the associations with the moon and thus the elements of water and the cover of darkness). Furthermore, its connection to the moon makes it great for specific types of healing, such as relieving PMS symptoms and assisting with hormonal imbalances. The moon's relationship with the feminine is undeniably important. The moonstone is also considered to clear the immune system and make a woman look younger when she wears it. The stone is also beneficial to pregnant women during pregnancy and labor. The use and wearing of moonstone can also help to improve female intuition.

Bloodstone

Bloodstone is a very dark green stone with deep crimson flecks running through it, giving it the appearance of being black. It is associated with the element of fire due to its rich color and red undertones, evoking passion and dispelling negativity. The bloodstone was supposed to be inured with Christ's blood in medieval times since he was injured during the Passion. For many, the stone became a hallowed object as a result of this. Bloodstone was worn in ancient Egypt to improve a warrior's strength and to make him invisible, diverting the enemy's attention away from him. Bloodstones purify the immune system, eliminating any physical or spiritual barriers, according to modern Wiccan practice. Its blood link persists, and it is regarded to be beneficial to circulation and excessive bleeding. It is frequently worn during childbirth to stop any bleeding that may occur, posing a risk to both mother and child, and it is also said to be a fortunate charm for preventing miscarriage while on display. A person who must go into war can also wear the bloodstone to defend themselves from injury in battle or to stop the flow of blood if they are wounded. It also boosts strength thanks to its ancient ties to Mars, the god of war. It can also be utilized to channel the energy and power of storms in weather magic.

Jet
Jet is a type of petrified wood that may be found all over the world and isn't technically a stone or a crystal. Jet is often regarded to be a potential aid in opening a gateway between realms because of its unusual physical and chemical features, as well as the fact that it is a product of both earth and fire. It was worn by the ancient Greeks to revere Cybele, a primal and powerful deity who was their interpretation of

the ultimate Mother Goddess. Jet was worn as a symbol of mourning as recently as Victorian times— its black color having been adopted as the right color for mourning in Western civilization—and Viking wives were said to carve protective symbols into jet for their husbands to wear while at sea. It is still widely utilized for protection, and is often placed on gateways to ward off evil spirits. Jet also possesses additional abilities, such as the ability to expel malevolent spirits and other beings that bring negative energy (psychic vampires, lurking demons). It can be utilized to open a portal between realms because of this power, but only with skilled practitioners and with extreme caution. It must be recharged after any strenuous ritual: bury it in the dirt for a few days for best results. It's also stated that giving jet to someone else, especially if you've worn it, is bad luck because it's thought to absorb a piece of your soul. Most certainly, this is not a property you want to give away. It can also be utilized to ease pain and reduce inflammation in the mind and body.

Tiger's Eye
The tiger's eye is a gorgeous stone with a striking golden core set against black, as its contrasting hues suggest. It holds the power of the earth and the sun. Since ancient times, it has been used as an ornament. The tiger's eye is a protective amulet that is also thought to aid bravery, therefore it was commonly connected with warriors and battles. The tiger's eye is an unavoidable element of your toolset if you're practicing natural Wicca in the spirit of conservation, as its obvious link to big cats suggests. Tiger's eye can also serve to ground the spirit and prevent addictive

behavior; it helps guide you away from intense desires to take unnecessary risks or spend recklessly. It's also stated that if you wear or carry a tiger's eye throughout the day, whatever deception you've encountered would finally come to light. It can also be employed in rituals to increase prosperity, thanks to its golden eye, which brings good fortune, and it promotes the flow of positive energy in general.

Lapis Lazuli

For thousands of years, this vivid blue stone has been utilized in the application of make-up and the wearing of jewelry. It was even reduced to a powder. Powder in beverages and potions supposed to boost stamina—an ancient Roman aphrodisiac that might also act as a poison remedy (a fairly frequent murder weapon during that time). A lapis lazuli ring was reported to be worn by Biblical King Solomon. Due to its color and delicacy, it is perhaps unsurprisingly connected with the elements of water and air. Lapis lazuli is thought to be extremely adept at severing the connections between the conscious and unconscious minds, therefore boosting intuition and feeling, as a very protective stone. It is thought to be a fidelity agent that is shared between partners and lovers, as well as a psychic link and healing agent. Its beautiful blue color soothes the nervous system and is very beneficial for eye healing and depression relief. While it is beneficial for healing, it should not be used in any food preparations because it is toxic—contrary to Roman usage in ancient times. Because sunlight might change the color of the stone, recharging should be done under the moonlight on a bed of pure quartz.

Other

The above list is only a partial one, of course, but these are some of the more common and more important crystals and stones that are used in Wiccan practice. The abundance and variety of crystals is nearly astronomical, and it can be stated with confidence that all earthly elements contain some sort of universal power, coming from the earth and imbued with elemental energy. To understand further how to use these crystals and stones, continue with the following chapters which explain the contrasting and balancing energies of stones, how to cleanse and recharge them, and how to use them in various ways, from altars and gardens to elixirs and talismans and beyond.

3rd Chapter:
From Projective to Receptive, the Magic of Stones

Stones have been used as sources of enormous power throughout human history, from productive tools to protective weapons. Stones may be honed and used to manufacture other excellent tools, build shelters, dress and chop meat, as well as protect, defend, attack, and hunt. They've also been utilized as magical artifacts throughout human history, which is understandable given how important and valuable they were to the development of civilization in general. Stones have long been utilized to connect humans to the physical domain of the ground and the spiritual realm of the deities, from the beautiful placement of Stonehenge's towering monument to the burial mounds seen in early Native American towns.

That is, stones are used in rituals that invoke both the earth from which they came (it's no coincidence that stone markers are still used to mark Christian graves ("ashes to ashes, dust to dust," as we return to the earth from which we came) and the deities who help us continue our journey beyond the physical realm. They were used to foretell the crop, divine the seasons, and tell time, among other things. Modern Wiccan practice recognizes that there is still something sacred in the stone and uses it to channel energy, connect to the divine, respect nature, and practice ritual and intent. The usage of stones in Wicca also complies with some of the fundamental precepts of Wiccan thought and practice, in that they contain both masculine and feminine energies, mirroring the balance between the spiritual realm's deities and the physical realm's elements. With their energies of fire and air (masculine) and earth and water (feminine), the Horned God and the Mother Goddess are co-equal deities of the spiritual realm (feminine).

As a result, stones conform to this cosmic equilibrium, with some signifying masculine potency and others female power, as well as one or more of the essential elements. We can also regard them as symbols for other powerful universal forces that function in harmony, such as the sun/light and the moon/darkness, or the yin and yang notions in Eastern philosophy. The divine, according to Wicca, may be found everywhere and through everything in nature; it does not exist apart from us or our natural environment. Its energy, on the other hand, works with and through us.

As a result, when we practice Wicca, we are channeling these many energies to assist us in achieving our goals and honoring the spirits and natural environment. To that aim, everything in the universe, including the very stones of the ground, is in balance with all other elements and energies. This balance is generally regarded as a balance between masculine and feminine forces inside our human standards of thinking—basically, a useful shorthand for understanding how and why the cosmos functions the way it does. However, according to Wiccan beliefs, these dualities are not absolute; that is, a balance of the two exists inside each of us and all natural components.

There is no such thing as a complete and absolute masculine, just as there is no such thing as a complete and absolute feminine: both work together to produce a bigger Universal All. Furthermore, reviving and revitalizing the feminine components of the natural and universal balance has been one of the aims of current Wiccan practice. That is, the masculine has had a position of privilege and power throughout history; Wicca, on the other hand, emphasizes the balance between the two, emphasizing that the feminine is just as primary and powerful as the masculine. This has been a method of restoring female images from those of the virgin or whore, Barbie doll or crone. It is meant to imply that the female's power stems from their fertility, which they use in conjunction with masculine energy to produce life, nurture it, and gain wisdom and strength in the process.

It's meant to imply that masculine connotations with financial success and professional dominance are incomplete without the feminine spiritual insight and compassionate sensitivity. Wicca envisions a balance of power between two deities, typically referred to as the Mother Goddess and the Horned God, rather than a single all-knowing and all-encompassing "God" figure. The cosmos would not be able to reach balance or wholeness without both. The Mother Goddess, like the universe, the seasons, and the phases of the moon, resides in a state of flux— another permanent tenant of Wiccan energy and practice. She is full of promise and fertile vitality when she is young, as in the springtime, an image of the virginal maiden playing in the field. When she is a mother, having reached the peak of her fertility, as in summer and fall, she nurtures and punishes in equal measure: remember, the universe is constantly changing. There are no absolutes in this world. But, tempered by the wrath that Mother Nature may occasionally unleash, this loving Mother Earth figure controls the sowing of the fields and the reaping of the harvest; she is vital to all life. She hibernates with the winter in her old age as the crone, bringing her wisdom near to her. She can be frigid and vengeful, like the howling winds outside, or brave and warm, relying on her wits to survive the slumbering earth's time. Despite this, she never abandons us, and each year, the regeneration of the seasons, the year's repeating cycles bring back this never-ending rebirth and eventual ending.

The Horned God also recognizes the Mother Goddess's intrinsic flux and dualism. He, too, has three phases: the young boy of the sunrise, full of promise (but also inexperience), the strong man of midday, brimming with confidence (if occasionally arrogant), and the old man of the setting sun, the hunted god who has given his all to the abundance of the harvest and now must be set aside for the nightly reign of the moon. The Horned God, in contrast to the Mother Goddess, who goes through a constant cycle of aging and regeneration, is depicted as a hunted animal who must die after freely giving all of his fertility to the fields and harvests. Of course, he regenerates in the same way that the Mother Goddess regenerates: their cyclical natures are identical, but their philosophical underpinnings differ slightly. They imbue the natural world, which we humans are an integral part of, with the essence of both the feminine and masculine. No matter how much we suffer under the weight of stereotypes, they are still with us as a means of comprehending the universe's complicated and contradictory character. Everything we do is infused with their spirit

.Essentially, all universal energy strives toward balance in Wicca and other pagan practice, and the usage of stones is most beneficial with a thorough understanding of the basics of this concept. Continue reading to learn about the differences between the two main energies of stones, as well as the appropriate applications for each.

Masculine Energy: Projective Power

The masculine energy of the universe reverberates via projective stones. They are powerful and active, causing movement and resisting inertia. Projective stones are more closely associated with the physical realm than their receptive counterparts, and they are linked to the fundamental constituents of the universe. They are hot stones with brilliant colors like orange and red, as they are made of fire and air. Because they—and their masculine energy—are linked to the sun, projective stones are frequently associated with vivid, flaming yellows and burnished golds. These stones are also associated with mental acuity and courage, as well as willpower and strength, and they have the ability to attract luck and success.

In essence, projective stones have all of the stereotypical male qualities that we often associate with them in most cultures around the world; however, in Wiccan philosophy and practice, they are inextricably linked to and balanced by the feminine energy found in receptive stones and their associated characteristics and powers.

Projective stones are utilized in some types of healing and protection from all kinds of negative energies— as well as in exorcisms to cast out evil influences. These can also be employed in rituals that promote self-assurance, good fortune, and resolve. These manly stones have a more direct effect on the conscious mind than on the subconscious, and they radiate a positively charged electrical energy. These are often tougher stones that can be used to sharpen tools and weapons, as they were previously employed to do so.

In alphabetical order, here is a brief but comprehensive list of projective stones:

- Agate with bands
- Agate (black)
- Brown Agate is a kind of agate.
- Agate (Red)
- Amber
- Apache Tear
- Aventurine,
- Bloodstone Calcite (Orange)
- Carnelian
- Cat's-eye
- Citrine
- Stone of the Cross
- Crystals of Quartz
- Herkimer Diamonds
- Rutilated Quartz
- Quartz Tourmaline
- Garnet
- Hematite

- Mottled Jasper
- Jasper, Red
- Lava
- Mica
- Obsidian
- Onyx
- Opal
- Pipestone
- Pumice
- Rhodonite
- Ruby
- Sard
- Sardonyx
- Serpentine
- Sphene
- Spinel
- Sunstone
- Tiger's-eye
- Topaz Red
- Tourmaline is a type of tourmaline that is found in nature.
- Zircon

Any of these stones can assist you with a variety of rituals while also infusing your surroundings with force and brightness. Keeping some on your person, atop your altar, at your home, and in your car is a good idea. These projective stones should always be available for use in your toolset for specific rituals involving specific aims.

Feminine Energy and Receptive Power

Receptive stones, in contrast to the projective strength of the previous stones, contain a wide range of feminine qualities and energy. In contrast to the physical character of projective stones, receptive stones are connected with serenity and spiritual aim. They encompass the potency of the moon, darkness, and the numerous animal and natural energies associated with such. It's no wonder that the feminine has always been prized in shamanic ceremonies and pagan traditions, as its spiritual link to other realms is stronger than the masculine's. Additionally, the feminine has been associated with animal familiars that wander, hunt, and exist in the dark across cultures and throughout history—the cat, the wolf, the bat, and others never fail to appear in literature and lore about witches and pagans. The original Dracula, a famous Bram Stoker novel, makes extensive use of these connotations to build his terrifying—yet alluring—figure of the night and the forbidden.

The projective stones, with their masculine energies, appear to suck up the strong rays of sunshine, whilst the receptive stones perform best in the moonlight. From the greys, blues, and silvers of the moon and her light to the soft greens and muted browns of the fertile earth, their hues represent the elements with which they are most typically associated. Pink is also associated with receptive stones and feminine energy, as its muted hue does not arouse the passions in the same way that a fiery red does. These stones represent the Mother Goddess's vitality as well as her elements of soil and water. These stones work inside and mystically, with magnetic rather than electrical energy, rather than being aggressive and energetic. Their mystique is similar to that of the moon phases, tides, and seasons—all of the gentler workings of nature that are both completely understandable and a little bit enigmatic.

Receptive stones, like projective stones, are employed in a variety of rites and practices. Receptive stones are ideal for meditation and divination practice because of their links to intuition. They can enhance psychic abilities and act more discreetly in the subconscious mind than in the conscious mind's brilliant regions. These responsive stones are employed in a variety of applications.

Love and compassion, empathy, and peace are all addressed in rituals and spells. They should be utilized to encourage spiritual growth by assisting a Wiccan in opening her mind to the universe's possibilities. These stones help the practitioner to be receptive to positive energy and spiritual entities, as their name implies. Even touching a responsive stone absorbs some of your anxiety projections, calming and easing you into a higher level of being. Because of their connection to the moon, they are also helpful in dream interpretation and in promoting restful sleep patterns. In contrast to the masculine's brittle mind, feminine energies are generally seen to be mystical and wise.

Receptive stones, like projective stones, rely on traditional feminine connections that have served us well throughout history and across cultures. They are utilized in conjunction with and as a balance to the projective, masculine stones in Wiccan ritual. This is in line with Wiccan views in general.

In alphabetical order, this is a partial but comprehensive list of responsive stones:

- Blue Lace Agate is a type of agate that is blue in color.
- Green Agate is a mineral found in nature.

- Moss Agate is a type of agate that has a moss
- Amethyst
- Aquamarine
- Azurite
- Beryl Calcite (blue)
- Calcite (green)
- Calcite (pink)
- Celestite
- Chalcedony
- Chrysocolla
- Chrysoprase
- Coral Stone of the Cross
- Crystals of Quartz
- Crystals of Blue Quartz
- Green Quartz Crystals are a type of crystal that is found in nature.
- Crystals of Rose Quartz
- Crystals of Smoky Quartz
- Emerald
- Fossils
- Geodes
- Holey Stones is a song by Holey Stones.
- Jade Brown Jasper (Brown Jasper)
- Green Jasper is a mineral that is found in nature.
- Jet
- Kunzite
- Lapis Lazuli is a type of lapis lazuli.
- Malachite
- Marble
- Moonstone
- Mother-of-pearl
- Olivine
- Opal

- Pearl
- Peridot
- Petrified Wood is a type of petrified wood that has been preserved over time
- Sapphire
- Selenite
- Sodalite
- Sugilite
- Black Tourmaline is a type of tourmaline that is found in nature.
- Blue Tourmaline is a type of tourmaline that is blue in color.
- Tourmaline
- Pink Tourmaline is a type of tourmaline that is pink in color.

Turquoise It's also worth noting that not all stones fall neatly into either the projective or receptive categories. Because stones are frequently made up of multiple elements, they might have qualities from both. Nonetheless, most stones have a dominating energy and should be used accordingly. It is also up to the individual practitioner to inspect and "feel" the stone for herself, determining the type of energy it emits. The following chapter will show you how to select the best stones and how to use them to your advantage.

4th Chapter:
The Best Crystals and Stones: How to Pick and Use The Best Crystals and Stones: How to Pick and Use

One of the most well-known types of Wiccan-based magic (or "magic," as it is frequently expressed) is crystal magic. Most Wiccans perceive these magnificent stones as more than simply physical expressions of elemental characteristics; they look to be alive and pulsing with energy. They communicate volumes about the heavenly mysteries and complicated energies that make up both the physical and spiritual levels, as they emerge from the depths of the earth. Learning to cast intentions and spells with crystals is an important aspect of most Wiccan practices. Recap the following to review what we've learned about crystals' basic qualities and how to use them:

- While not all "crystals" used in Wiccan magic are truly crystals, the majority are minerals of some form, thus the term is a handy shorthand. One of the most popular is quartz, which is a genuine crystal, followed by rose quartz and amethyst. Lapis lazuli, bloodstone, and jade are some other crystals that are frequently utilized. There are an endless number of crystals (and stones) that can be utilized in Wiccan magic and ritual once you get past the basic stage. A more detailed list can be found in Chapter 2.

- Crystals' energy resonates with their power: they are thought to have healing properties, and some crystals even emit an electric charge. Crystals are uniquely tuned to the essential energies of the universe because they are so connected to the earth, and so to the Mother Goddess. There is no greater substance through which to channel our thoughts—our intentions—from the physical to the spiritual planes since our thoughts—our intentions—are actually energy.
- Crystals are frequently used to indicate the boundary in casting a circle, offering both protection and an energetic area for successful magic and ritual. They can also be utilized to boost intentions during rituals or prayer, as they have the ability to magnify any intention transmitted. They can also be utilized in certain spells, the most basic of which is to empower a crystal with purpose during a ritual and then take it with you to manifest it. They're also commonly utilized as talismans and amulets.

Crystals for cleansing It's just as vital to know how to use them as it is to learn how to use them. This is why it is usually preferable to locate a location where you can choose your crystals.

person. Even among the most basic crystals, such as pure quartz, you will notice that one shines out above the rest. The energy inherent within crystals attracts us, and it is well worth your time and effort to spend time not only looking at but also holding and investigating them. If a crystal doesn't communicate to you, it won't be able to channel your energy and intentions as effectively. The link between the user (the Wiccan) and the tool is where the magic happens (the crystal).

However, you can find crystals and stones in a variety of places, from New Age shops to flea markets to (in certain cases) large box stores. It's also a good idea to look about on local sites or social media to see if there's a Wiccan coven or pagan group in your region; if there is, this would be a great place to start looking for the greatest availability and cost in your area. If you can't find your crystals locally, there are a plethora of websites and companies online that sell crystals, stones, and other Wiccan tools and equipment. Do your homework in this case: prices range from wholesale providers who sell a big quantity of random crystals at a low price (but with uncertain quality in many situations) to specialty shops that sell ready-made amulets and jewelry alongside their crystals for normally higher costs. If you have to buy something online, make sure you've done your homework and checked to see if the company is reputable—and if they offer a decent return policy.

 If you receive a batch of faulty crystals or stones—or knockoffs of what you truly want—you'll want to know that you'll be able to return them. Amazon also sells crystals and stones, and while it is a massive corporation—not exactly in line with a Wiccan nature mindset—it is a respected company with good return procedures.

In any event, the price and quality of crystals and stones, as well as the energy they emit and how they connect with you, differ significantly. At the end of the day, it's always best to try to find them in person. There are even spots where you can find your own stones: keep an eye out for fascinating stones and other items when traveling—you never know what you'll find. When cleaned and analyzed, that unappealing mud-colored stone could turn out to be a valuable piece of carnelian, for example. There are even spots in the country where you may go crystal-digging for yourself, such as the Great Salt Plains in Oklahoma's panhandle or California's Himalaya Mine. In reality, similar sites can be found in practically every state in the nation; a little internet research can help you find the one closest to you. Some of these require a fee to dig or search; others merely charge a fee to enter a nearby state park; and others are completely free. But, if you can find it, digging out your own prized crystals and stones to utilize in your daily practice is the ultimate experience.

Crystals are being charged is the first step in efficiently utilizing them. After you've purchased your crystals, make sure to cleanse them before putting them to use in your practice. This involves the basic process of washing them—a symbolic act of purification—as well as the art of releasing any negative energy or past vibrations that might interfere with how you intend to use the crystals.
Give your new crystals a thorough, cleansing bath, and if they're discovered crystals, tumble and polish them as well. Simply wash them in a warm water bath with a small amount of neutral detergent, then soak them for at least an hour in clear, cold water. If possible, dry them in the sun; this is especially crucial for crystals connected with projective, fiery energy, which is obtained in part from the sun. Allow your crystals to dry naturally in the open air whenever

possible. It's also crucial to cleanse your crystals with moonlight; this is especially vital for receptive crystals that acquire a lot of their energy from the moon and feminine energies. However, all crystals can benefit from receiving some charge from both the sun and the moon; as previously said, many crystals have projective and receptive elements. As a result, exposing all crystals to some energy from the sun and moon increases their potency and strengthens their spiritual links. If you're concerned about leaving stones outside due to your location, place them on an open windowsill where they may absorb sunshine and moonlight. This should leave them shining and attractive, purified, and ready to use for the most part.

One word of caution: some crystals are quite delicate, and exposing them to abrupt temperature fluctuations, intense cold or heat, or leaving them out in the elements can cause harm. When cleaning and washing crystals, exercise prudence and common sense. Excessive exposure to light can also result in the formation of some crystals.

stones to deteriorate as well. Although salt is commonly used as a purifier, it can damage the surface of softer crystals, so proceed with caution.

Smudging crystals isn't always a good idea, for the reasons cited above: it can damage or discolor them. Other methods for cleansing crystals include immersing them in a herbal bath with herbs that are typically used for purification, such as sage (smudging crystals isn't always a good idea, for the reasons cited above: it can damage or discolor them). Burying your crystals in the dirt is a very deep technique of cleansing: if you bought them from a source you don't know much about, this may be the best approach to assure that you're properly purging the crystals of undesirable energy. If you can, bury them in the roots of a tree or plant, and label the spot so you don't lose track of where they are. Allow them to rest for a full moon cycle for the most thorough cleansing; however, even a few of days will suffice. For a quick cleanse before each ceremony, employ the cleansing breath: simply inhale a deep breath, infuse it with good intentions and energy, and blow onto the crystal before use. This is also a way to keep your connection to your crystals strong.

Keeping crystals safe also takes some consideration and comprehension. Even those who don't use crystals or stones in rituals must think about how to maintain them looking beautiful (indeed, one could say, everyone who collects these specimens has some awareness of their energy, or they wouldn't be drawn to them in the first place). Even if you don't use your crystals every day—you'll probably wind up with a few favorites in heavy rotation and the rest doing occasional duty—they should be kept safe and secure.

The first factor to consider is the fragility of the crystal or stone: some crystals would collapse if not handled carefully, others might be scratched or fractured, and still others are as tough as boulders. Sort your crystals by fragility first, ensuring that the most delicate ones are kept in a secure location where they won't be knocked or thrown around.

Next, sort your crystals by color to determine if they are projective (red, orange, gold, for example) or receptive (green, blue, purple, etc.). (Blue, grey, light green). As the crystals sit together, they can also draw energy from one another.

The location of your crystals has a significant impact on how you utilize them: some will invariably remain on your person, whether as jewelry or tucked into a pocket or purse. Just make sure they're safe when it's essential. Others will remain by your bedside, beneath a pillow, or propped upon your workstation; just keep in mind that they will need to be recharged from time to time in order to continue channeling good sleep or productivity, and so on. You'll almost certainly store some on your altar, which is another spot where you'll need to consider about replenishing from time to time. You can also scatter the crystals throughout your home, remembering the cardinal directions and the energy that each crystal represents. This creates an entire environment in which the crystals communicate with nature and spiritual forces, as well as with each other and your energy and intentions, in order to ignite the flow of energy throughout your home. Look at feng shui principles for ideas on how to generate this flow, then move on to the following chapter for more specific suggestions on how to set up your crystals for certain rituals and everyday use.

5th Chapter:
Organizing and Maintaining Good Power with the Crystal Configuration

Once you've accumulated a certain number of crystals, you may start thinking about how to best use and channel their energy in your home and daily life. Carrying specific crystals with you, strategically arranging them on your altar, organizing them throughout your home to promote the flow of energy—all of these ideas are excellent methods to get the most out of your crystals outside of specific rituals and spells (which will be covered in the latter half of the book). However, there are some other methods for increasing the strength and reach of your crystal collection, including organizing crystals in certain ways to achieve specific intents. Careful organization and tidying areas are important components in having a cleansed and energy-focused Wiccan house, thus this should also be a priority when arranging and preserving your crystals. The following suggestions include some basic ideas for organizing your crystals and keeping your practice meaningful, as well as two more thorough suggestions for creating a highly strong crystal arrangement.

Altar of Crystals

Once you collect enough different types of crystals, you can easily create an altar for them. This can be kept on your main altar or in other place of your home that you think is suitable for long-term display and use. The following suggestions will assist you in getting started on this worthwhile undertaking. This altar is a physical manifestation of your spiritual practice, and as such, it provides a serene and potent space to which you can return each day.

❖ The following are some easy altar-building tips: Using materials and arrangements that make sense and feel right to you, trust your intuition and set it up. Take your time to arrange it in a way that appeals to you and gives you the most energizing feeling. It's best to put up the altar during a new moon, when the atmosphere is conducive to new aspirations. Finally, maintain the area clean and uncluttered; don't disrupt the energy by allowing clutter to accumulate around the shrine.

❖ Make a special location for yourself that you consider sacred and receptive to positive energy. It's not a good idea to build your altar on a hill.

❖ floor, which denotes a lower importance, such as tossing something carelessly to the ground. A elevated surface of some kind displays lofty ideas and goals better.

❖ Clean with zeal whatever surface and place you intend to use. You want to create a powerful area where the most vital of goals are broadcast throughout the universe and met with equal force. Make careful to dedicate your altar to a specific purpose. This can be whatever your specific goal is at the time. It can be for a specific purpose, such as finding love or attracting good fortune, or it can be to aid your meditation or ritual practice; it can be to honor your patron deity or a vital element, or it can be to commemorate a season or Sabbat. Of course, the longevity of the altar is determined by the goal, but the notion is that the more focused the intention, the higher the return on the outcomes.

❖ Select your gems with care, though this should go without saying, and remember that this is your personalized altar, so feel free to add anything that feel right to you to the arrangement. Candles, herbal bundles, and symbolic things can all be placed on this altar, but the crystals should be the focal point. To keep your altar's focus clear, you can place written intentions and/or affirmations on it judiciously. It's also crucial to use natural materials as the altar's foundation, such as a fossilized wood slab or a wooden board.

❖ To increase the altar's effectiveness, consider the cardinal directions and their correlation with the primary elements (north/earth, south/air, west/water, and east/fire). After you've completed all of this, be sure to use your altar, whether it's for mindful meditation, occasional ceremony, or simply to observe and touch each morning before you start your busy day.

Grid of Crystals

Creating a crystal grid is another technique to organize your crystals so that their potency and energy are maximized. A crystal grid, unlike an altar, is made entirely of crystals, which are put in a careful pattern to conduct and enhance various types of energy and intentions. It incorporates sacred geometry as well, so that the pattern is part of the grid's potency. The techniques for constructing a crystal grid are identical to those for constructing a crystal altar, with the exception that it is made entirely of crystals and depends on pre-determined patterns rather than intuitive combinations.

❖ You'll also need appropriate stones for your purposes and a crystal to function as your central point, from which all energy radiates outward, in addition to picking and purifying the optimal location for your crystal grid. In order to activate your grid, you'll also need a pure quartz point, and while a crystal grid cloth with design guidelines isn't required, it's really helpful, especially for your first effort.

❖ First, choose a specific desire or objective to manifest, just like you would with a crystal altar. Make sure you have enough appropriate crystals to fill your grid in accordance with your objective. If you're aiming toward abundance, for example, you'll want to choose stones that correspond to prosperity and good fortune energies, such as jade, citrine, and pyrite, which are green and gold stones. Choose stones that specialize in healing, physical energy, and sound sleep if you're focusing on health and wellbeing. A rather thorough list of stones and their qualities may be found in Chapters 2 and 3.

- On a piece of paper, write your purpose clearly and set it in the center of the grid, underneath your central crystal. Arrange your crystals in the grid, beginning on the outside and working your way to the center, while thinking clearly or gently about your desire or aim. Last but not least, place your Centre crystal.
- Finally, activate your crystal grid by drawing a line connecting all of the stones to each other and to the center crystal with your pure quartz point, starting from the outside and working inward. This helps to materialize their energy and awakens their purpose of collaborating on your specific goal.
- You may make any number of crystal grids, from a prosperity grid to a protection grid to a willpower grid—the only restrictions are your own intentions and aspirations. There are several graphic examples and step-by-step directions to setting up on the internet. crystal grids in particular To make a health and wellness grid, for example, you'll need/can use a Flower of Life crystal grid cloth, twelve fluorite stones, six sodalite stones, four each of yellow jasper and turquoise stones, two aventurine stones, and your central crystal and pure quartz point, as well as your central crystal and pure quartz point. This is a good place to start when making a basic crystal grid.

Ideas for a General Organization
- Keeping a journal is a good idea. This is also advised for general Wiccan practice, whether it's a handcrafted Book of Shadows or a grimoire, and it may be used to keep track of what crystals you have and how you've used them, as well as recording the outcomes as you progress. This can be highly useful in

determining which crystals are functioning best for you, as well as noting which crystals you do not yet have but intend to obtain for future intentions and rituals.

❖ You may also make a crystal chart, noting which crystals are appropriate for specific purposes, as well as whether they are projective or receptive, masculine or feminine, and/or which essential components they belong to. This could also include notations on each crystal's distinct characteristics and/or an assessment of a stone's specific color, energy, or chakra.

❖ For your crystals, you can either build or buy unique shelving. Leave crystals out for show and safekeeping rather than putting them in a box or pouch all the time. This also allows you to arrange the stones in such a way that they support and conduct each other's energies in more strong and effective ways. It's also useful for recharging crystals: simply move the shelf with the crystals to a windowsill during a full moon, as all varieties of crystals benefit from some moonlight recharging. Consider the overall shape— square or oval, regular or irregular—that would provide the most energy boost to your collection, as well as the inside configuration, with wider slots for more significant or physically more remarkable stones, when commencing on such a project. Customization is preferable than homogeneity.

❖ If buying or making custom shelves isn't feasible due to cost or time constraints, carefully place crystals in a bowl or bowls for display. Consider it in the same light as arranging them in bespoke shelves; that is, arranging them so that their energies coincide, and placing particularly powerful crystals in the center so that their energy radiates outward to all the other specimens. Consider the balance between projective and receptive stones, as well as their color attributes and magical properties. You should use a natural material, such as wood or clay, for your bowl or bowls (bamboo, that endlessly renewable resource, is another increasingly affordable option). Look for a container that communicates with you in the same manner that your crystal does; it should have its own energetic signature to add to your collection.

❖ You might also consider displaying your collection in a terrarium, in addition to bowls. Terrariums provide a way to arrange your crystals utilizing all of the ideas above but with the added benefit of holding them in a more structured setting and keeping them free of dust and debris. They're not a bad idea to keep in a Wiccan home, either.

❖ If you have an outdoor space, it wouldn't be out of place to put some of your crystals there as well. Placing crystals outside your living space, whether it's a garden, a front or back porch, or even an apartment terrace, is a fantastic method to channel positive energies into your home while repelling negative energies. If you happen to come across some really large crystals, this could be the ideal location for storing and utilizing their energy. Protective stones, as well as any other crystals with which you have infused specific intentions you intend to bring into your life, are excellent choices for this type of arrangement. Of course, this affords regular opportunities for crystal recharging, so after you've found a configuration you like, consider swapping out individual crystals so that your entire collection can receive moonlight and other direct natural energy. Consider how you'll build up this arrangement, then continue on to learn more about the potential for stone gardens in the next chapter.

❖ Finally, if you accumulate so many crystals that you can no longer keep up with daily display and dusting, some basic but clever boxes are not to be overlooked. Choose lined boxes with transparent compartments for various stones, both for the stones themselves and for the stones to be stored in. Physical protection, especially for delicate stones, as well as spiritual energy preservation. Furthermore, boxes with clear covers are available for this type of storage, allowing you to readily peep at your collection whenever you choose.

In essence, there are a plethora of methods to organize your collection in order to optimize its potential and power. Pick the ones that work best for you and your environment, and use as many as you like. Crystals play an important role in any Wiccan's practice and everyday life.

Surround yourself with as many people as you can and appreciate them as much as you can.

Chapter: 6
The Stone Garden: Organizing and Maintaining Good

Organizing and caring for your crystals and stones doesn't have to be limited to the indoors; in fact, building an outdoor location where you can practice in general or hold rituals and celebrations is a perfectly acceptable and pleasant way to immerse yourself in Wiccan practice. The ability of stones to direct, conduct, and amplify energy is undeniable, especially when they are charged and assembled with deliberate care on a regular basis. Communicating with nature and recognizing the essential elements should be a part of every Wiccan's everyday life, as it is one of the central pillars of Wiccan practice. Setting up an outdoor setting that blends the broad concepts of Wicca with the potent natural magic of crystals and stones is one of the greatest ways to do this, short of creating an outdoor altar or partaking in Dionysian type rituals (though both are also appropriate). The following suggestions will help you visualize how to set up that space, including how to incorporate and arrange crystals and stones in a natural setting to produce positive energy throughout your home.

Wiccan Garden Power Stones and Crystals
❖ Using stones and crystals in your garden is an absolutely suitable and effective approach to direct terrestrial energies: because these things are made of the earth, it's only natural that they respond and

speak with it, acting as a conduit between your desire and the natural universe. Crystals and stones can have an impact on the health and abundance of the organic materials you plant; one approach to help your garden thrive is to use them to stimulate growth and avoid sickness.

❖ Green and brown stones, which symbolize the earth element and are so closely associated with the concepts of gardening and harvesting, are among the most suitable stones for your garden. These stones indicate riches and stability, as well as growth and rejuvenation. Smoky quartz, pyrite, tiger's eye, and petrified wood are wonderful alternatives for grounding your garden, while emerald, jade, bloodstone, green fluorite, and green calcite are other fertile choices. Citrine, amber, and gold topaz are examples of yellow stones that are associated with the sun and provide success and confidence to your endeavor. Water is represented by blue or grey stones.Bring a soothing, calm element to your garden with moonstone, turquoise, azurite, and lapis lazuli, as well as the associations with the magical powers of the moon.

❖ Take into account the stones' appearances other than color, such as their condition or state, and their geometric configurations. Considering whether a stone is tumbled (that is, polished) or rough, for example, has an affect on its use: Tumbled stones are common in Wiccan practice, from meditation to healing to protection, and beyond; raw stones are theoretically more delicate, but they can also be more powerful and connected to the soil from which they came. There are other geometric shapes to examine, such as whether a stone is in the shape of a pyramid (suggesting spiritual reach and amplification), spherical (suggesting infinite access to energetic flow), or cubed (suggesting limitless access to energetic flow) (suggesting mindfulness, willpower, and concentration). These factors will aid you in selecting and arranging stones that are actively working to actualize your goals.

❖ The following are some examples of stones that are widely utilized in gardens due to their unique associations:

- Moss Agate, often known as "the gardener's talisman," is a common sight in alternative gardens. It encourages healthy plant growth in a wide range of species.
- Tree Agate is utilized to boost your garden's energy field's sense of security and stability. The Tree Agate is a symbolic guardian of your garden and space, much as trees are symbolic protectors of the planet.
- Green Aventurine absorbs negative energy, bringing peace and shielding a room from pollution's detrimental impacts.
- Aquamarine is utilized to harness and boost water's positive properties, which helps to alleviate drought (also especially good if you have a water source in your garden, such as a natural pond or water barrel).
- Green Calcite is regarded as the "encouragement stone" because it can help relax your plants and surrounds, promoting a thriving, serene garden.
- Citrine is a happy stone that resonates with a lot of energy and warmth.

- Rhyolite is a mineral that promotes toughness and fortitude, and it would be very beneficial to any struggling garden. Pure quartz, of course, is the master stone and may be used in practically every situation, as a master healer and positive energy conductor.

❖ Use any number of ways to arrange your crystals and stones in obvious patterns in your garden. Arrange stones in accordance with the four cardinal directions, with the elements of earth, air, water, and fire representing north, south, west, and east, respectively: see Chapter 3 for an orientation in the varied energies and alliances of particular stones. Alternatively, make a grid design with stones and crystals, with a powerful core stone radiating outward to link to an encircling arrangement of carefully picked stones; this can resemble any number of Wiccan symbols or be something entirely new.

❖ You can also utilize your stones as garden guardians, arranging them around the perimeter of the space in the same way that you would a circle around a sacred space for ceremonies.

❖ Consider storing stones in the watering can to lend positive energy to what's growing, or hanging stones on tree branches for protection. To facilitate the passage of energy between the living space and the garden space, line the pathway with stones and crystals.

❖ Of course, gardens are always seasonal to differing degrees, but consider your stone garden—or the space within your garden dedicated to stone arrangements—as a way to recognize the various seasons throughout the year by establishing color and shape patterns that match to each season. The four elements and cardinal directions could also be used as a guide. Your Mother Goddess homage may take the form of a herbal garden with green stones indicating fertility and brown stones honoring the earth; it would be gorgeous even in the middle of winter, only waiting for the rebirth of spring to become full and active once more. A central stone grid can also serve as a guide for what to plant and how to arrange it. A stone garden might, without a doubt, serve as a form of shrine where you can pray.

❖ perform rituals in nature; this, of course, depends on you and how much privacy and space you have. Finally, you might simply create a stone garden and let nature take its course; that is, a stone garden is powerful even if organic materials are not planted, however a combination of organic and inorganic energies is certain to resonate with greater energies.

General Wiccan Garden Ideas

❖ The perennial magic of nature, of the garden or outdoor space that you may cultivate, may be the first focus. Consider the benefits and possibilities of using a harmonious garden space: nature is magical, and by creating a conscious space in which to practice Wicca and understand the connections between all living (and, in the case of stones, inorganic but energetically charged) materials, one can engage in some of the highest magic. A garden can provide herbs that are frequently used in Wiccan spells and rituals, as well as harnessing the renewable energy of the earth and plants in a variety of ways. It can also create an even greater sense of interconnectedness by arranging organic and inorganic materials in specific ways to promote specific energies and intentions. Consider the garden to be a spiritual workshop for you.

❖ A garden is both a planned and an unplanned space: on the one hand, you're carving off a specific place for specific reasons, just as you would for your altar indoors; on the other hand, you're also honoring nature's accidental unpredictability and the inherent power within that entropic energy. Set apart and clear a space, sure—smudging is especially useful in creating a garden area—but don't forget to enjoy the wildness of nature's response. Weeds will sprout in between your nicely set stones no matter what you do. Keep everything as tidy as you want or can, but accept the inherent abundance of life.

❖ When establishing an outdoor place for a Wiccan lifestyle, don't just throw away the stones and other components you find when clearing your space; use them to create the grid and perimeters of your garden. These objects will vibrate with local energy and reverberate in your area in ways that store-bought items will not.

❖ You can encircle your sacred space with found stones, be they large or plentiful enough; place them at the corners of your property representing the four cardinal directions for protection and the encouragement of energy flow; or plant them purposefully in the ground before an image of the deity to whom you pay homage, depending on what you find. Use that energy to conduct positive vibrations and concentrate magical potential using found stones and other natural items that have a natural link to that location.

- Consider the power of intentions in words themselves, in addition to purifying the area through a combination of purification rites and smudging. To eliminate negative energy, start by sprinkling water—spring, not tap—mixed with some lemon (juice or extract) across the garden space. Then, to attract favorable energy, sprinkle spring water mixed with rose scent. Smudge with natural herbs (sage is a good choice for this type of energy), then think about what you want the space to be and how you want it to actualize your wishes. To bless and inure the place with meaning and intention, say a brief invocation (you can write this yourself or do a quick internet search for some ideas). Carve intention and affirmation words into the stones you'll use in the garden, or plough them into the soil. It's all about matching the energy of your desire and intention with the natural energy that exists in and flows through your garden space.
- By resting your hands on the earth, you can also communicate your intentions—and your potential healing power—to the ground that you have cleared for your sacred practice. Simply place your palms flat on the earthen surface or on the face of a stone and repeat your desire; your hands should get warm as a result of the energy flow you create in collaboration with nature spirits.
- Dance and incantatory prayer can also be used to achieve this form of blessing and sacrament. This type of energy exchange can be very effective when done under the light of the moon.
- Plant herbs and other flora with magical properties, such as Artemisia silver frost or select tree kinds, in addition to your stone setup. There are several

flowers that are thought to have magical abilities, the rose being one of them. Moon gardens are also worth considering: there are a variety of plants and flowers that bloom there.

❖ In connection with the Mother Goddess, these plants are said to be exceptionally potent and auspicious when seen under the moonlight. Magical herbs have a wide range of applications in Wiccan practice, and many of them are simple to grow at home (both indoors and out), making them all the more powerful within your space because you planted your intentions alongside the seeds or seedlings. Seeds can be employed as magical artifacts in and of themselves because they are very symbolic of the ritualistic cycle of renewal and rebirth.

❖ All of the aforementioned activities have the added benefit of attracting birds and bees. Aside from their obvious connection to fertility, both birds and bees have a long history of magical mythology and many forms of good luck and energy. Part of the purpose of developing the garden is to provide a habitat for living organisms.

❖ Consider other natural, mostly "found" objects that can have profound ties to natural and spiritual realms, in addition to stones. While stones are naturally associated with the earth element, shells are related with water, sticks are associated with fire, and feathers are associated with air. When you combine all four elements in your garden, you get a powerful force of energy.

❖ Finally, practice asking for permission. Make sure to communicate your objectives to the finding things and see how they react; this takes time and experience, but it's a crucial element of becoming a responsible and strong Wiccan. Understanding that the natural world reacts in the same way that a sentient being does is crucial to harnessing and recognizing that power. Always express thanks to the earth or the element from which you are drawing energy and intention, whether by a simple thought intention or an offering of water, food, or a personal item. This understanding fuels and sustains the spirit of connectivity that exists between our individual selves and the natural, spiritual world that surrounds and nurtures us.

7th Chapter:
Essences and Elixirs in Practical Magic

Crystals are essential in the manufacture of a variety of other therapeutic potions that can improve health and well-being in a variety of formulas, in addition to channeling energies and directing intentions via altar settings and personal adornment. The manufacture of elixirs, or tonics, and essences is one of the most common uses for crystals in Wiccan practice. An essence works by imprinting the energy of a specific crystal in water, converting the crystal's vibrations into something that can be consumed; it is the crystal's essence. An elixir is a more intricate potion made by combining crystal essences with other substances. Making and drinking elixirs is an important aspect of Wiccan practical magic, as it promotes diverse purposes and provides healing balm.

The Crystal's Essence is its core

The essences of certain crystals are used in all crystal or gem elixirs, sometimes in combination with other ingredients. Making an essence is rather simple, though there are some fundamental rules and suggestions to follow, and there are other locations where you may buy prepackaged essences and elixirs if you choose. Crystal and mineral essences and elixirs have been used for ages by people from all walks of life. To encourage good fortune and longevity, the Chinese mixed spring water with the essence of jade, while ancient Greeks and Romans drank powdered minerals in their beverages to cure a variety of ailments. Epsom salts and powdered tinctures, for example, are still utilized to treat the body and mind today. The use of earthly elements in the practice of healing and well-being promotion is nothing new or uncommon.

It's easy to create an essence: Choose a crystal with the energy and attributes you want to use; make sure it's cleansed and charged. Place it in pure water (spring water, fresh rain water); let it to absorb sunlight or moonlight for a whole day or night, depending on your objective; then utilize. Sunlight is thought to be best for physical and material goals (physical healing, prosperity), whereas moonlight is better for emotional and psychic goals (love, divination). For the process, make sure to utilize a non-reactive container, such as to keep out external contaminants, place it in a glass and cover it tightly. You should also examine a variety of other aspects that may have an impact on the quality and power of your essence, including as the season, weather, location, and time of day, as well as how they interact with your intention. Although an essence can theoretically be generated at any time and in any location with practically any intention, the effectiveness of the essence will surely be increased when these other aspects are considered and employed intelligently. You can also improve the quality of an essence by creating it with ritual purpose, which means using your altar, forming a circle, and using all of your magical abilities to make the most potent essence possible.

These essences can then be combined with other essences to make an elixir (more on that below), or they can be consumed directly by ingesting the water or applying it to the body. However, many crystals and stones can contain toxins, so drinking essences if you're not sure about the toxicity of the crystal you're using isn't a good idea. This is why many Wiccan practitioners obtain essences from reliable suppliers.

Still, with practice and some knowledge, you should be able to make your own essences.

There's also indirect infusion, which is a safer option: the crystal is placed on a clear barrier between itself and the water, and its energy is imparted more delicately to the water without it coming into direct touch, reducing the risk of hazardous poisons being absorbed. If you're new to Wicca, this is probably the best technique to make an essence. Some may argue that indirect immersion results in a less potent essence; however, there are two simple things you may do to eliminate this argument: First, utilize clear quartz as a barrier because it is known for being highly conductive of all energies; second, extend the infusion period to allow the crystal energies to be absorbed into your water supply.

Elixirs are magical concoctions

Now that you've got your essences, you may start making elixirs and using them for a variety of purposes and in a variety of ways. An elixir can combine two or more essences to make a personalized blend for whatever goal you're pursuing; it can also add other elements that boost the energy of the crystal essence while also improving the flavor. Plants and herbs soaked in water or alcohol are another type of elixir that can be combined with crystal essences, honey, and/or other ingredients.

Spices are added for flavor, but they also have their own strong characteristics that can be used for a variety of purposes. Essentially, you decide how to make an elixir for your objectives, and there is no one-size-fits-all recipe for any reason.

However, there are some guidelines to follow in terms of what to use for what purpose and how to consume the elixir. The following are some of the most often utilized crystal essences, along with their properties:

❖ Aphrodisiac properties of agate
❖ Amethyst is utilized to bring tranquility to oneself or others.
❖ Citrine is a stone that promotes personal transformation and power.
❖ Fluorite promotes spiritual transit and communication across realms.
❖ Hematite is utilized for grounding and steadiness.
❖ Jade is a stone that encourages peace and kindness.
❖ Lapis lazuli is a stone that promotes mental and emotional clarity.
❖ Obsidian assists you in breaking harmful habits.
❖ Clear quartz stimulates the flow of energy.

These are only a handful of the more common stones and crystals used in elixir-making, and they can all be combined to make a potent elixir for a variety of purposes.

Elixirs can be taken internally in the form of drops (three to eight, depending) applied under the tongue or infused into filtered water for drinking (again, apply caution as noted above). The dosage and duration are usually determined by the essence utilized and the desired intention: the higher the energy contained in the crystal, the lower the dosage and duration. Crystals that are red and orange, projective crystals associated with male energy, should be used in lower numbers because high energy crystals tend to exist on the red end of the ultraviolet spectrum. Yellows and greens in the middle of the spectrum are considered neutral energy, whereas crystals with blue and purple coloring and tremendous receptive energy at the violet end of the range can be ingested in higher doses. Furthermore, the length of time each elixir should be taken varies: the greater and neutral energy, lower dosage elixirs can be used on a regular basis, with a seven-day break every two weeks for high and every month for neutral. Lower energy elixirs are not recommended for long-term use due to their greater dosages; use every other day.

During the duration of a month to be clear, these are not FDA-approved suggestions, and using any mineral essence or elixir directly should be done with prudence and common sense. There are, however, other applications for elixirs that go beyond direction consumption.

For one thing, you can use a dropper or a small spray bottle to apply an elixir externally. This avoids direct intake while targeting the specific location of the body on which your intention is focused. Nonetheless, it is a process that should be approached with prudence and care. You may also use elixirs to promote abundance and fertility in plants and herbs by infusing a few of drops in a spoonful of water and sprinkling around the base of the plant for a week or two. You can also use crystal elixirs in your bath water to promote healing and well-being; a few drops in a full tub should suffice and pose no safety risks.

Finally, elixirs can be used in conjunction with other Wiccan practices: they can be extremely useful in clearing negative energy from a space; apply with a spray bottle in a circular pathway through the space, keeping doors and windows open if applicable, to promote the dissipation of negative energy and the increase in the flow of positive energy. They can be sprayed on surfaces to cleanse and rejuvenate in combination with ritual practice at your altar. They can be employed to increase devotional energies and worship the deities during specific Sabbats. In a nutshell, elixirs are useful tools to have on hand for almost any Wiccan activity.

Use of Potions in General

The Wiccan toolset includes a variety of drinkable potions and clever brews in addition to crystal essences and elixirs. These are a slightly different category, as they occasionally use crystal essences or rely on crystal energy to be most effective. This is presented here as a basic summary of the various types of Wiccan magic available to practitioners; for more detailed information, see my other works, Wicca Book of Spells and Wiccan Herbal Magic. Other types of handmade magic are briefly described in the list below.

❖ Magical potions, particularly love potions, have been prepared for a long time and have become legendary. Honey, rose water, and other basic components are still utilized in these types of potions today.
❖ verbena. Additional herbs, plants, and spices are used to make a variety of other potions.

❖ Witch's brews are another mythical substance that has earned a bad rap over time but is still utilized and can be very soothing, therapeutic, and energetic. Some ordinary liquids, such as beer, coffee, and tea, are technically brewed and can be considered to have magical characteristics; many types of fermented beverages have been and continue to be utilized in ceremonial rituals of many kinds. There are also other types of brews, such as broths made from a combination of vegetables and herbs to promote various health advantages. For example, a fantastic witch's brew—normally called stew—can be made by blending carrot (for luck), onion (for protection), potato (for soothing), and beef (for vigor) with a little water. When produced with intention and ceremony, and consumed with intention, this can be just as potent as any elixir in terms of magical effectiveness. Add some therapeutic herbs and you've got a delicious supper with a wide range of benefits.

❖ Other liquids, like as wine, have long been regarded to have magical characteristics and have been utilized in ritual rites throughout history. Whisky, as well as other varieties of beer and mead that have been barrel fermented or aged, are frequently used in rituals and festivities. Why do we name them spirits, do you think? They were utilized to communicate between the moral and spiritual realms, as well as to invoke the deities.

❖ Wiccans also prepare infusions, which can be a tincture of herbs and leaves to make an infused tea, or an infusion of herbal oil or vinegar to add to food or drink to improve health and well-being. You may also use crystals and other natural items to infuse water with various energies to use in your laundry wash, bath, cleaning, and other household activities.

❖ Keep in mind that anything that comes from nature has a magical quality to it and is endowed with universal energy; hence, plants and herbs, foods and beverages, minerals and elements all have capabilities that can be used to materialize purpose. The universe is saturated with magical material to produce all kind of essences, infusions, and elixirs, from the purifying nature of the lemon to the soothing beauty of honey to the vibrating energy of crystals.

8th Chapter:
Talismans and Amulets in Practical Magic

Talismans and amulets have been found throughout history, attracting positive energy in one case and protecting against negative energy in the other. A talisman is a magical object—often, but not always, formed of crystal or stone—that has the potential to attract tremendous forces in the universe, allowing for healing, nurturing good fortune, and promoting fertility and plenty. An amulet is a form of talisman that is nearly always made, at least in part, of crystals or gemstones and is used solely for protection and defense. A casual understanding of the phrase talisman in reference to Wiccan and other magical practice might suggest that it is a type of good luck charm, such as a rabbit's foot keychain or something similar, however actual talismans are things holding potent magic and substantial energy.

The exact differences between talismans and amulets are still debated, but most experts agree that a talisman is a more powerful object because it contains both the inherent power of the materials from which it is made as well as the power imbued by the Wiccan or other practitioner who magically charges it. Because of its exceptional strength, some believe that a talisman's power can be passed to other elements, things, and even humans. An amulet's power originates from the substance it's made of; it's composed of crystals and stones that already have defensive properties, and it becomes an amulet after a Wiccan gives it that intention. In either instance, talismans and amulets are frequently worn on the body to boost the user's energy and intention.

Talismans and amulets emerge throughout history in numerous cultures and retain significance in many, while the usage of the amulet appears more frequently—in tough times, in a pre-scientific world, protective stones had a plethora of purposes. In ancient Egypt, for example, they were frequently utilized to ward off black magic and evil eyes. Egyptian tombs are brimming with numerous gemstones and crystals that were thought to aid in the afterlife's transit. There are numerous stories in Greco-Roman mythology concerning even titans and gods wearing protective amulets: When Prometheus steals the gods' fire and gives it to man, he wears a sapphire ring; Orpheus brought an agate stone with him when he descended into the underworld; and wearing a magnetite amulet was considered to make the voyage into the underworld easier. In the middle Amulets were used to guard against animal stings and bites in Eastern cultures, while talismans were used to promote good fortune in the Far East.

From Roman soldiers to Viking raiders to Celtic tribesmen, it has long been customary for warriors of all kinds to wear amulets of diverse meanings and materials. And accounts of numerous rituals and amulets used to protect them on what was then a dangerous journey abound throughout sea-faring societies. This tradition has a long history, halted only by the Christian church's assertion that it is incompatible with God's ways. Despite the church officials and parish priests' prohibitions, crystals were still displayed outside homes and worn by people during the Middle Ages and plague years in an attempt to fend off the dreadful sickness.

As a result, the use of talismans and amulets is still embedded in our cultural imagination—does anybody remember Stephen King and Peter Straub's collaboration novel The Talisman?—and Wicca has resurrected its use and significance for modern practitioners.

Attractive Auras Talismans

Talismans work by attracting positive energy and manifesting a specific set of objectives on behalf of the Wiccan who created it. Creating a talisman entails two steps: first, you must choose the right material for the talisman you want to make, and then you must figure out how to best empower that talisman with the most powerful magic. In the first situation, you must comprehend how distinct crystals and stones function, as well as the types of energy and attributes they possess (see Chapter 2 for a partial list and Chapter 3 for an understanding of projective and receptive energies). Every characteristic of a crystal is important for its use as a talisman: its crystalline or elemental structure, which endows it with specific energy; its shape, which influences how energy flows through it; its color, which links it to specific elements (earth, air, water, fire); and its connection to the user herself. In the second case, you'll need to figure out how to best empower the crystal or stone to attract the energies you want: carving an incantation or spell onto or around it; setting it into jewelry to wear close to the body; charging it with specific energies designated for the intention; pairing it with numbers and patterns that produce a certain conductivity to the spiritual realm. These are the fundamentals of talisman creation.

Refer to Chapters 2 and 3 for more information on which crystals and stones are suitable for which goals, but keep in mind that other materials, particularly in the construction of talismanic jewelry, can contribute their own energy to the development of a talisman. Gold and silver represent prosperity and protection, whereas iron represents strength and protection. Aluminum is utilized for communication and is lucky in travel, while copper is used to foster love and is helpful for healing. Various plants also have qualities that can be used in the creation of the talisman as well as in its purification and charging. The forms and colors of the materials you're dealing with should also be taken into account, as they have their own unique qualities.

Activating a talisman might be as simple as blessing it at your shrine or reciting an incantation with a specific goal in mind. To guarantee that your talisman is blessed with the most potent of energies, perform a full-fledged ritual: light a candle and incense at the altar, indicating the powers of fire and air, and have a chalice full of water and a bowl full of salt available, symbolizing the powers of water and earth. Start facing north, holding the talisman over the salt, and reciting an incantation calling the north; then repeat facing south, holding the talisman over the candle flame, then facing west and east, holding the talisman over the chalice and incense smoke, respectively. Declare the purpose of your talisman after you've finished invoking the four elemental spirits and their cardinal directions. This turns it on for a while, but it will need to be recharged after that.

Shields of Protection: Amulets

While talismans are more intricate manifestations of magical intent, an amulet is just as powerful and significant. In reality, most of our talisman legends are passed down through the generations through the use of protecting amulets. An amulet is used to protect against negative energies or defend against unwelcome events, whereas a talisman is used to attract certain energies (disease, invasion, accident). An amulet is basically just the sum of its parts: a specific crystal or stone with some form of protective energy, instilled with a specific intention by a Wiccan practitioner through a ritual like the one described above. Amulets are frequently worn or carried. Depending on the exact purpose, they can be tacked to doors, hung from trees, or buried in the ground.

Indeed, the applications of amulets were very specific in ancient times, and protective crystals were supposed to have unique protective properties. The seafaring Greeks, for example, devised a classification system consisting of seven different stones that were useful for voyages: A garnet stone was considered to protect seafarers from drowning, whereas pure quartz warded off severe weather, aquamarine warded off fear, and coral warded off the ship itself. Jet provided total protection when traveling on water, and banded agate protected against storm surges. Plain agate was used to defend against evil spirits or negative energies that might rise up from the sea or be carried in by the winds, in an attempt to ward off the evil eye. All of these stones are still used for protective amulets and defensive spells, and they can undoubtedly be utilized in the way they were meant.

Consider the shape of your amulet in addition to the mineral it is made of: spherical amulets are regarded to be more powerful since the spherical shape encircles the intention—as does casting a circle in ritual practice in general—and represents an energy that has no beginning or end. The circle, in essence, cannot be broken. Spherical shapes are frequently compared to eggs, which serve as natural defenses for the delicate babies inside. Crystals and stones cut or sculpted into specific shapes have a powerful aura of authority, as seen by their historical use in crowns, scepters, and other authoritative power trappings across cultures.

General Usage Advice

While the information above should get you started in your hunt for the perfect talisman or amulet, here are some more suggestions for how to use and strengthen them.

❖ Generally speaking, you should employ the talisman that you produce. Making a talisman for someone else is a bad idea because the energy is unique to your abilities and intentions.

❖ Furthermore, the more knowledgeable you are with the qualities of the substance you are working with, as well as the symbols and runes you employ to further empower that material, the more successful the outcomes will be. Making a powerful talisman necessitates a significant amount of time and work.

❖ Having said that, it is absolutely appropriate to add your own personal lore to the talisman—an inscription of your own creation, a symbol of personal value, or a pattern that reflects something meaningful to you. It's necessary to channel energy through established runes and symbols, but it's also important to create your own traditions based on your own particular experience and energy field.

❖ If you're going to wear the talisman or amulet, think about where it should go. Wearing a talisman on a necklace close to your heart, for example, would be a good way to draw love energies, while embedding an amulet in a headband or hair accessories would shield you from mental attack. Of fact, merely having a talisman on your person, whether in a pocket or a purse, can be useful, but not as specifically directed.

❖ Tattoos are indeed used as talismans and amulets in numerous civilizations. The energy you want to attract or the protection you want to create can be etched onto your body, which has a talismanic impact.

❖ Consider where the greatest area to use your talisman is if you aren't wearing it: strung on a tree limb outside your house to keep negative energy at bay; pinned to a child's bed to ward off evil spirits; buried beneath the garden to bring abundance and fertility Consider how the intention is related to the ideal area for channeling it.

❖ Patterns of letters and numbers are also supposed to attract positive energy while repelling bad energy: one such device is squares of numbers that match lucky numbers 15 or 18 travelling any direction, or patterns of letters that spell the same phrase across and down. Palindromes made up of letters arranged in a pyramid are likewise said to be talismanic. To endow a potent ingredient with even greater potency, these patterns can literally be carved into the surface of particular materials.

❖ Finally, many modern Wiccans consider the pentacle to be the most effective talismanic symbol. It captures the principles of Wiccan belief with its encircling five-pointed star: the four lower points of the star correspond to the four essential elements as well as the four cardinal directions, while the four upper points refer to the four cardinal directions.

❖ The spiritual dimension is represented by the fifth and highest point. The star is then encompassed by the universe's interconnected and unbroken energy.

9th Chapter:
Baths are an example of
practical magic

Crystals are not only excellent sources of energy for rituals, elixirs, and talismans, but they are also excellent sources of energy and healing for personal self-care. Taking a ritual bath with crystals and stones can be a magically significant method to recover from physical disease or emotional trauma, reconnect with your magical internal energies, or simply cleanse yourself after a long week of unpleasant energies and events. In a nutshell, it's like going to the spa, but with a more profound, long-lasting effect and a greater connection to a higher purpose. The following points will walk you through the different ways that ritual bathing with crystals may be one of the most fulfilling Wiccan activities.

❖ You may incorporate crystals into your bath in a variety of ways. The first and most obvious approach is to simply immerse crystals in the bathwater while bathing. However, because crystals might include poisons or dyes, this is not the only method to use them in the bath, and it is not always the ideal option. For another example, you can use powdered crystals in the bathwater or add a crystal essence or elixir (see Chapter 7). Finally, you can simply bring crystals into the bath with you, preferably in a significant design. As with any crystal ritual, make sure the crystals are clean, cleansed, charged, and ready to use.

❖ Be conscious of the crystals you choose and why: consider not just the specific intentions you want to manifest, but also the specific energies emanating from the crystal on that given day.

❖ Just because a crystal has a strong presence at your altar doesn't guarantee it will have the same radiance when you think of taking a bath. Hold the crystal in your hand and pay attention to how its energy responds while you think about your intention. Some practitioners will directly ask the crystal whether it wishes to take part in the rite. It doesn't matter which methodology works best for you, as long as you choose carefully.

❖ However, it's perhaps more crucial to check whether the stone is safe to use in the bath—if it isn't, go back to step one.

❖ suggestions. As previously stated, many crystals contain colors or poisons that make them dangerous to use in bathwater, while others are too delicate to be submerged in water. Any type of quartz (pure, rose, smokey), amethyst, citrine, and carnelian are examples of common crystals that can be used in bathing rituals. If you bought your crystals from an unknown shop or internet source, you should always examine them for chemical additives, such as dyes. Many commercial crystal distributors may color them to make them appear brighter and "better." The simplest approach to check this is to submerge the crystal in a glass of warm water for a few minutes and watch if the water changes color to match the hue of the stone. If you accidentally immerse yourself in bathwater with a crystal and see that the water begins to take on the color of the crystal, get out immediately and properly cleanse yourself.

❖ The crystals mentioned above are commonly used in the following ways:

- Pure quartz is a versatile crystal that enhances the energy of any other crystal it is combined with. In any case, having one or more of them on hand is a good idea. Rose quartz is thought to be a good conductor of self-love and a way to concentrate your energy on improving other love relationships in your life.
- Smoky quartz aids in the removal of undesired energy as well as the absorption of bad influences.
- Amethyst enhances your intuition while also assisting you in breaking harmful habits and reconnecting with the spiritual realm.
- Citrine attracts abundance and assists you in achieving your goals.
- Carnelian increases motivation and determination, and it can help to strengthen the relationships between soul mates.
- ❖ There are a variety of additional crystals that can be used in bathing rituals, whether in the water or as a support system around you in the bath. While bathing, you can also use candles and incense to boost the flow and intensity of energy; essentially, this allows you to wash more deeply.
- ❖ to bathe with all four primary elements, figuratively speaking Our crystals represent the ground, the candle represents fire, and the incense represents air, and you are submerged in water.
- ❖ Outside of the bath, place crystals that promote psychic ability or emotional well-being near your head, some around your center for grounding and physical health, and still others near your hips for active stimulation.

❖ Also keep in mind that crystals are temperature-sensitive: if you merely drop one into boiling water, it may split or become damaged. Instead, submerge the crystals in cool water and gradually warm it up over time while monitoring their progress. Some crystals may break even if the water is progressively heated. If this happens, preserve the crystal for another ritual since it will maintain part of its potency even if it is damaged. The crystals described above should be reasonably free of this issue.

❖ It is entirely up to you to decide how many crystals you utilize. If you're new to this, start with just one or two crystals; some individuals report that the energy of the crystals mixed with the conductivity of the water is overwhelming, leaving them feeling drained or dizzy rather than invigorated. So, start small and work your way up once you've gotten a sense of how you're feeling. You can also consider the power of numbers: three and seven are commonly regarded to be powerful magical numbers, however you may have a favorite or lucky number of your own.

❖ Don't underestimate the strength of internal intention. A ritual bath should, of course, calm and comfort you, but you should also be directing your intention into the energy you've produced with the things you've chosen.

❖ After you've done your bath, make sure to rinse and dry your crystals thoroughly before putting them back in their place. They'll also need to be recharged following the bath's intensity, so utilize one of the ways outlined in Chapter 4 to do so (recharge in sunlight or moonlight, bury in salt or earth, use clear quartz for re-amplification).

❖ Finally, here's an example of a particularly potent ceremonial bath. Gather three pure quartz stones, one citrine stone, a bay leaf, and a half cup of honey combined with two cups of milk. Place the crystals in the container.

❖ when your tub is about halfway full, add the milk and honey mixture to allow it to warm and mix with the rest of the bathwater; when your tub is about halfway full, add the milk and honey mixture to allow it to warm and mix with the rest of the bathwater; when your tub is about halfway full, add the milk and honey mixture to allow it to warm and mix While the bath is full, write your intention or a suitable sign on a bay leaf and float it on the water's surface. Spend at least 20 minutes in the bathwater visualizing your goal and how you'll feel after it's realized. You can certainly use candles and incense if you want to.

Remember that self-care is one of the most important things you can do for yourself, despite the fact that it is typically associated with indulgence and excess. Allowing oneself to become too exhausted, physically or emotionally ill to care for yourself depletes your vitality, making it impossible to care for anybody or anything else. The ritual bath is not an indulgence; rather, it is an act of empowered self-care, a way to re-energize your general health and well-being by recharging your spiritual batteries. This type of self-care should become a part of your powerful Wiccan practice on a regular basis.

10th Chapter:
Crystals and Candles for
Practical Magic

While crystals are potent in and of themselves for Wiccan practice, when paired with candles, their power is amplified. As a result, many objectives are manifested when crystals and candles are used together. Candles are particularly efficient at enhancing the strength of other objects because they can represent all four elements—the base of the candle representing earth, the flame representing fire, the wispy smoke indicating air, and the melting wax symbolizing water. In a very basic way, crystals represent the Mother Goddess, the element of earth; hence, combining candles and crystals creates an atmosphere in which the most profoundly felt intentions can be met. The next sections look at several strategies for exploring and manifesting diverse intentions.

Grounding

Wiccan practitioners are known to perform grounding rituals on a fairly regular basis. The reasons for this are both personal and universal: many people feel overwhelmed or harried in their daily lives, and thus find that grounding rituals help to re-center their emotions and spiritual skills. It's also true that, for the majority of human history, we've lived in close proximity to the earth—walking around barefoot, farming it with our own hands, relying on its bounty—and that we need to reconnect with it in some way, especially when following Wiccan beliefs. As a result, a grounding ritual might become a regular part of your routine.

❖ Light a natural, earthy-scented candle (sandalwood, pine, cedar) in a container that similarly reflects the soil, such as a brown or green natural wood holder. Hold a crystal in each hand; choose one or two that have earthy properties and grounding abilities, such as tree agate, moss agate, bloodstone, garnet, smokey quartz, or hematite. Consider how the candle's aroma and the crystalline structures of the stones are luring you down to the earth. Inhale the earth's forces into your body, and exhale any negative energy you may be sensing. Imagine yourself rooted to the earth, striving towards the very center of the earth's vitality and force; continue your journey by breathing gently and steadily. Once If you want to feel more grounded and linked to the earth's core, take a deep breath in the earth's energy. Continue until you feel stable and anchored. It's ideal to let the candle burn out completely on its own in this—or practically any other candle-related rite.

Health

The promotion of health and well-being is one of the most important aspects of Wiccan practice. There are a plethora of healing spells and rituals, medicines and elixirs to keep your constitution strong, and self-care festivities galore. When you start to feel the beginnings of an illness, such as a seasonal cold or cough, you should do the following to strengthen your immune system and get your body back on track before it becomes entirely compromised.

❖ Use a eucalyptus-scented candle for this activity, as it helps to clear the sinuses and open up clogged air passages. Place a carnelian stone at the base of your throat while inhaling the aroma of the candle. Breathe deeply until the candle goes out, focusing on your health and well-being. For a few more days, sleep with the carnelian stone under your pillow until your immune system returns to normal.

Love

The term "love" is broad enough to embrace everything from romantic love to platonic love to self-love; there's also the love you can cultivate via unprompted generosity and random acts of kindness. Another important aspect of Wiccan practice, fostering love, should be a part of your spiritual routine on a regular basis. The following gives you a basic overview of how to employ candles and crystals in manifesting love; to orient the process toward a specific kind of love, modify your choice of crystal—clear quartz for general expressions of love, rose quartz for romantic love—and candle kind.

❖ For this intention, light a rose-scented candle. Hold it close to your heart, infusing it with your love energy, while holding a crystal in your palm, allowing communication to flow between candle, crystal, and you. Self, crystal, and While holding on to your crystal, light the candle and envision yourself being slowly wrapped by a giant bubble of love, and that the sacred area in which you cast your intention is encased in a field of love. Take that offering of love into your body when you inhale, and eliminate negative insecurities and hostility from your innermost self when you exhale. Keep this field going till the candle goes out. After then, keep the crystal on your person if you want to develop self-love, or give it to someone else if you want to generate romantic or platonic love.

Joyfulness
While pleasure is incorporated inside the spirit of love, it can also evolve into its own unique energy, infusing the material and spiritual worlds with a sense of transcendence and happiness. When you look for joy, you're looking for a selfless connection to the world's limitless energy and potential, both physical and spiritual. Here's one way to channel that happiness and infuse it into yourself and people around you.

❖ Because you're harnessing the pure energy of sunshine, light a candle scented with a bright yellow or orange citrus aroma, then carve a sign of joy onto the candle for added effectiveness. Place four sunstones in each of the four cardinal directions surrounding the candle, as well as four clear quartz crystals in the same cardinal directions but a little further away from the central candle. The goal is to encourage joy to travel from the candle's center via the sunstones and out into the world, magnified by the quartz. Consider the candle to be the sun, with its beams shooting outward to provide joy to you, your area, and the world. Express appreciation to the four directions and the sun deity when the candle burns out.

Abundance

As with love, abundance can have many different meanings: it might represent success and fortune, or it can mean a spirit of richness and plenty that has to do with life in general—for example, harvest in ancient times.

particular. The following ceremony can assist you in bringing this energy into your life, regardless of your specific objective.

❖ Have plenty of crystals on available for this ceremony, which involves forming a crystal grid around a central candle: use clear quartz for amplification and citrine to represent the energy of wealth (and/or other stones that indicate good fortune, such as jade). Place a jasmine-scented candle in the center of the grid and keep it there while infusing it with your goal. Arrange your crystals in a circle around the candle, with the citrine closest to the candle and the quartz further away to radiate the energy outward. Allow the candle to slowly burn out while you send out the intention of abundance into the universe.

Success

Again, the term "success" can refer to a variety of situations, ranging from financial to relationship to emotional. However, in the sphere of Wiccan practice, what matters is what it means to you, because it is your purpose to bring about the kind of energy that determines your sense of success. Creating the spirit of success, then, is all about generating the energy that fuels your desire to succeed—however you define success. This ceremony will assist you in generating that energy.

❖ Use a cinnamon-scented candle—the more natural the better, such as anointing it with essential oil or dusting it with ground cinnamon. Choose and charge eight crystals with your goal to create success: carnelian, citrine, jade, onyx, and green aventurine are good choices. Light the candle and arrange the stones in a decorative, circular arrangement around it (think about which stone to place next to which, in terms of the amplification and transference of energy). On a Sunday, the symbolic start of the week and a subconscious invocation of the sun, this is a particularly opportune moment to do so. Make sure your candle and crystals are in direct sunlight, and concentrate your intention toward them as well as upward toward the sun. Concentrate on how success looks and feels to you. Keep the stones with you after the flame has burned out, in a pocket or a bag.purse, and carry it with you for the next week to bring prosperity with you wherever you go.

ESP

(ESP) is a term used to describe a person's ability to this isn't to say that you should go through a procedure to miraculously grant you ESP or telekinesis abilities; rather, psychic ability refers to the talent and openness required to communicate with forces beyond the physical sphere. That is, you are requesting the power to allow spiritual energy to flow into and through you, allowing you to comprehend the cosmos on a level beyond the physical. Here's one way to get in touch with those mysterious energies.

❖ A white candle perfumed with vanilla is used in this ritual, which is similar to meditation. Sit in front of the candle, concentrating on the flicker of the flame—call it a magical dance—while clutching a piece of amethyst infused with your goal. Start with a short candle to ensure that you can sustain your meditative state until the candle burns out naturally; progressively progress to longer-burning candles to increase the energy that your ritual generates. This is a method to tap into a deeper intuitive sense by relaxing into the flow of energy that is coming your way. You can eventually use this practice for divination by asking a question, especially one about direction, and then letting the answer come to you while you stare into the flame.

Assistance with Sleeping

When you don't get enough sleep, it's tough to channel positive energy; thus, if you have occasional or chronic insomnia, there is one practice that can help you get a good night's sleep without anxiety or nightmares.

❖ Chamomile is a well-known sleep aid in tea and other infusions, so start your ritual with a chamomile-scented candle. Lay down or take a contemplative pose and lay a blue agate or blue calcite crystal in your lap or in your center for serenity, then inhale deeply the aroma of chamomile, focusing your intention on relaxation and rest. Alternatively, brew a cup of chamomile tea before lighting the candle and sip it carefully as the candle burns out and the crystal emits calming energy. After you've finished the routine, make sure to take a moment to relax. Take the crystal to bed with you and place it beneath your pillow for a restful night's sleep.

Stress Reduction

Following one of the suggestions in the previous chapter for taking a ritual bath is one of the greatest, most calming, and fulfilling ways to relieve stress in your life with candles and crystals. Use lavender-scented candles and amethyst stones, as well as whatever else you think is appropriate for your own particular practice. Imagine all of your worry dissipating and going down the drain once the candles have gone out and the stopper has been unplugged. This ritual will quickly become a regular in your routine because it is refreshing, cleaning, and revitalizing all in one.

Chapter: 11
Crystals and Herbs in Practical Magic

The combination of crystals and herbs is a fantastic proposition, just like the combination of crystals and candles. These two substances, both from the earth but inorganic and organic in nature, can combine in powerful ways to provide protection, create loving energy, and free us from negativity. The healing abilities of herbs are enhanced by the crystalline energy of stones, resulting in improved efficacy in all types of herbal mixtures and treatments.

Herbal magic is one of the most practical forms of Wiccan magic because it uses activities that most of us are already familiar with and requires no special ingredients. Herbal magic has been used all over the world since the dawn of time, and it is still quite popular among Asian countries and indigenous peoples all over the world. Indeed, some of our scientific canon's most potent medications are sourced from common plant sources. Even in science-based civilizations, the belief that herbs have magical properties is not far-fetched. The Wiccan approach to herbs aims to improve our understanding of plants and increase the range of applications we can use them for. Herbs can be turned into strong therapeutic medications instead of delectable cooking staples.

When any of these are combined with the power of crystals, the result can be indisputably powerful.

This highly charged interaction has a wide range of applications, many of which are listed below.

❖ Crystals and stones, as detailed in Chapter 6, can be quite beneficial in the creation of a successful garden. Two of the most useful stones in gardening are moss and tree agate stones. These agate stones are claimed to strengthen the attunement between human and plant consciousness, allowing for a greater, more positive flow of energy between the two. They work on both the gardener and the garden itself. When you meditate outside with either of these stones, you can get more connected to the earth element in general. In the second scenario, these stones will boost the garden's yield by protecting seeds and boosting growth. This can be accomplished by placing stones at the base of plants or by using a combination of methods.

❖ surrounding the garden's border; you can also construct a modest altar of stones in the garden's center, allowing the energy to radiate outward. Infusing the water that you use to water your garden can also help to increase yields and promote positive energy.

❖ Plants in general have communicating abilities that are beyond our comprehension. Plants communicate through a number of mechanisms, including roots and fungus, blooms, and seeds. Plants have evolved to reproduce their species and defend their territories without the use of limbs or central nerve systems, thanks to their exceptional symbiosis with other species (plant, animal, mineral). We can learn a lot from them about how the broader universe functions in interdependent harmony. Herbs are a convenient method to claim a portion of that energy, imbue it with intention via crystals, and practice self-healing.

❖ Making herbal tinctures and teas with crystal essences—water infused with the energy of certain crystals—is another approach to combine the energies of crystals and herbs (see Chapter 7 on how to safely make essences and elixirs with crystals). This improves the viability of your brew for healing, love, or whatever other goal you're attempting to achieve. To aid with headaches and migraines, use a rose quartz infused essence in a love potion, or a lapis lazuli charged essence in a lavender tea. Any energy or desire you have in mind is amplified by clear quartz, as it always is. To improve the efficacy of your herbal medications, you're essentially combining earth elements with water.

❖ Crystals are also commonly used to raise psychic and spiritual frequencies, which can be done in conjunction with connecting to plants and nature in general. Leave stones as offerings to the spirits at the four cardinal directions within the garden; focus on your wishes and detect the flow of energy between yourself and the plants if your garden begins to exhibit indications of disease or suffering.

❖ Crystals can also be used in herbal smudging ceremonies. Build a modest stone altar with a clear quartz anchor and a cast of tourmaline or obsidian around it; carefully light your dried herb bundle (sage is generally at the top of the list).

❖ Imagine receiving the energy from the stones up via your herb bundle and wafting it through the room (make careful to have a fireproof anchor of some sort underneath it for safety). This procedure cleanses the region of negative energy while also infusing it with the grounded earthen energy of the crystal altar. Essentially, you're removing the negative and channeling the positive.

❖ Use dried herbs and flowers, such as lavender and rose petals, to make a cleansing face steam. Place two clear quartz crystals (or one clear and one rose, for love) in a wide bowl, then arrange your dried herbs and flowers around them—a variety is best, but the two ideas above will suffice. Pour a large amount of very hot water over your face—be sure to choose crystals that can survive high temperatures—then lean over, covering your head with a towel to keep the steam from escaping. This is a cleansing and invigorating weekly beauty routine with plenty of positive energy.

❖ Sew little crystals and herb bundles into the seams of your apron for culinary work or into the pockets of pants or overalls for outdoor labor in the garden or otherwise to preserve and promote good energy as you work. Select stones for good fortune and abundance, and herbs such as basil for protection.

❖ Herbs can also be used in your crystal cleansing baths, as well as in your everyday shower: hang a bunch of fresh herbs—rosemary, lavender, and mint—along with some fresh eucalyptus fronds from your shower head. These will cleanse your crystals as well as whatever goal you have for them during your ritual wash. Depending on how fresh they are and how damp they become, these can linger in the shower for several days to weeks. When they've lost their freshness, recycle them into your compost pile. Return all of that energy to the earth!

❖ Use obsidian and bay leaf to connect with your ancestors (this is only one possible combo, but it's a nice one): Place the bay leaf outside beneath a full moon and write a sign on it that represents a specific ancestor or simply invokes ancestral spirits. Allow it to rest until the moon has diminished to its lowest point. Tiniest crescent, concentrating on the ancestral powers you'd like to connect with every night

❖ Herbs are perfect for making sachets, dream pillows, and homemade incense and oils, among other magical items. When these are combined with crystals, their potential magic is amplified: Keep an amethyst under your herbal dream pillow for extra psychic energy; use a cut crystal as an incense holder. To begin using herbs in regular Wiccan practice and occasional ritual or celebration, you merely need to research and comprehend the varied qualities and energies held by various herbs. For specific information on which herbs to use where and how to use them successfully, see Wicca Herbal Magic: Perform Rituals with Wicca Herbal Magic, Flowers, and Essential Oils.

❖ You can also achieve remarkable results by combining crystals with essential oils made from botanical items. Essential oils can be infused at home or bought from a variety of retailers. Here are some suggestions for suitable pairings of the two:

• Spray grapefruit oil on a citrine stone and place it on your altar or another conspicuous point in the house to promote optimism.

- Anoint moonstone or jade with bergamot oil to boost self-esteem; this brings uplift and confidence. A wonderful method to use this combination is to anoint a piece of moonstone or jade jewelry with bergamot oil (jasmine also works) and wear it until the aroma fades. If required, recharge your crystal and repeat.
- Purify some lace agate with lemon or peppermint oil to enhance physical energy; the combination of stone and oil boosts energy and desire for exercise. This would be a wonderful spot to keep these amplified stones if you have an exercise room or a designated duffel bag.

- Anoint malachite with peppermint oil (or vanilla essence—not a real essential oil but also appropriate) and keep it on your dinner table to encourage healthy eating.

- Peppermint oil is both invigorating and a natural hunger suppressant, while malachite encourages good change. Spray jasper with orange oil and carry it in your pocket or purse to induce happiness. They both infuse your vitality with the exuberant thrill of sunlight.
- Sunstone can be infused with essential pine oil to help you reconnect with nature. Of course, you can't be outside if you can't be outside, such as during the worst winter storms or when you're locked in an office. This is a great item to keep on your desk to remind you of nature.
- Use ylang-ylang oil to anoint a garnet to improve romantic or platonic relationships. This encourages a relationship's bond to become stronger, and it's

especially wonderful as a present for a partner or friend with whom you want to form a stronger bond.

- Spray jasper with rosewood oil to encourage a sense of service, since it reminds us that our worth is derived from what we offer to others and fosters sentiments of empathy for others.

- Anoint moss agate with marjoram oil to foster thankfulness. The former conjures up happy recollections, whilst the latter keeps us grounded and in check.
- Use frankincense to anoint turquoise to improve psychic connection. This is a common healing combo that also promotes spiritual openness.

❖ The potent mix of crystals and herbs (together with their accompanying elements, plants, and spices) can even assist us in breaking bad behaviors like addiction (to smoking, drinking, eating, and so on). Combine equal amounts of cinnamon, ginger, and chili powder in a large fireproof pot—or cauldron, if you have one—and place on top of a piece of charcoal. Place a red candle on one side of the pot and a black candle on the other; surround the pot with citrine, amethyst, and/or clear quartz. "Red is the color of strength, red is the color of power," repeat a chant as you light the red candle, admitting that red is a strong, powerful hue. Day by day, hour by hour, I have the strength to break this habit." Then, using the black candle, ignite it. "Black is the color that sends things away, and gives me the power to kick this today," she says, referring to the hue's ability to repel negativity. Then, once the spice/charcoal pile is properly burning, drop it upon anything that represents the unhealthy behavior or addiction you're trying to break (part of a cigarette pack, food or alcohol wrapper, or even a piece of paper with the habit written and crossed out). Allow that to burn out while the candles do, then smudge the space with sage.

Conclusion

Wicca is, in the end, a powerful way to reconnect with nature and energy in order to release positive forces into the world. Its open and fluid attitudes appeal to a wide range of people, and its belief systems are geared toward empowering women and promoting self-care. Wicca supports a practice that is egalitarian, rich in process, and filled with gratifying ritual and community, based on the belief that the goddesses are equal to the gods, as well as an acknowledgment of the importance of natural forces.

You've joined the vast world of Wiccan crystals, which comes with a set of beliefs, rituals, and traditions that have swept the Western world since the mid-nineteenth century. The usage of crystals is one of the most important aspects of Wiccan practice: these ancient products of the earth and its essential elements are curiously alive, channeling energy from all realms. Wiccans use crystals for a variety of purposes, including cultivating love, generating positive energy, and providing protection. With their potential to link to global forces and bring them into your house and heart, gemstones and other stones are also important components of Wiccan practice.

Wicca is an inclusive belief system that emphasizes our connections to the natural and spiritual realms, with crystals serving as a fundamental conduit between them. In Wiccan practice, the Mother Goddess and the Horned God infuse their vitality and knowledge into our daily lives. Anyone who wants to channel their energy into a positive and strong life of intention and achievement can start by developing a crystal grid, a stone garden, or nurturing a collection of powerful and healing crystals to help them in their daily lives.

CPSIA information can be obtained
at www.ICGtesting.com
Printed in the USA
LVHW082141240822
726827LV00025B/584

9 783986 532123